More I Jesus

Developing the Fruit of the Spirit in Your Life

SELF-CONTROL

JOY

GALATIANS 5:22-23
BUT THE FRUIT OF THE SPIRIT IS
LOVE, JOY,
PEACE, PATIENCE,
KINDNESS, GOODNESS,
FAITHFULNESS, GENTLENESS
AND SELF-CONTROL. AGAINST
SUCH THINGS THERE IS NO LAW.

© 2000, Ben Steed.   http://www.heartlight.org

More Like Jesus

Developing the Fruit of the Spirit in Your Life

A Six Week Spiritual Journey
for the Thirsty Soul

SUZANNE NTI

Published by Fresh Manna
Milton Keynes, UK

More Like Jesus

Published by FRESH MANNA
P O Box 5083
Milton Keynes MK7 7DU
info@freshmanna.org.uk
Tel: +44 (0)1908 528441
Fax: +44 (0)1908394752
www.freshmanna.org.uk

Correspondence Address:
P O Box 5083
Milton Keynes MK7 7DU
snit@freshmanna.org.uk
First edition 2005

ISBN Number: 0-9549721-0-4

Printed and bound by Antony Rowe Ltd, Eastbourne

Find us on the World Wide Web at
http://www.freshmanna.org.uk

CONTENTS

KINDNESS & GOODNESS

FAITHFULNESS

MEEKNESS

SELF CONTROL

DEDICATION

I dedicate this book first and foremost to God who owns my life.
To Jesus Christ, my Lord and Saviour through whom I have
received an absolutely fantastic overcoming life, eternal benefit and
retirement plan.

To Danni, the husband that God gave me knowing just what I
needed when I didn't.

To the children God blessed me with, Rhema, Rock, Aman and
Judah who are helping the cultivation and development of the fruit
of the Spirit in my life.

To all my beloved brothers and sisters in the Lord who have helped
me make it this far.

FOREWORD

Many people who are born again and Spirit filled have neglected to develop a personal relationship with their heavenly Father. They have remained content to belonging to the family of God and serving Him collectively through ministry.

God desires you to know Him intimately - to take on His nature and character.

Because of His love, the Father yearns for His children to begin to cultivate every fruit of the Spirit - to conform to the image of Jesus.

It is a blessing to see my book being used with the excellence, time and work Suzanne has put into it for the building of God's kingdom. Christians who follow the biblical principles set forth in my book, the 'Call for Character', broken down into this six week journey 'More Like Jesus' will be recognised as those professing Christians whose lives truly emanate the Christ-like qualities of love, joy, peace, longsuffering, gentleness, goodness, faith, meekness and temperance. (Gal 5:22, 23) All disputings over the controversial doctrine of the Holy Spirit must stop here, for against such character qualities, who can argue?

I encourage every Christian who with a good and honest heart desires the manifestation of the fruit of the Spirit in his or her life, to read this book with an open heart - to be willing to receive all that the
Holy Spirit has to offer - especially the character of Jesus.

- Greg Zoschak

INTRODUCTION

When I became a committed Christian I found that although I had become a new creation spiritually, the nature of Christ which came as a result of the indwelling of the Holy Spirit was not very evident in my life. I expected the fruit of the Spirit to just begin to automatically manifest in my life from the start. Instead I found that the works of the flesh that Paul describes in Galatians 5:21, "sexual immorality, impure thoughts, eagerness for lustful pleasure, idolatry, participation in demonic activities, hostility, quarreling, jealousy, outbursts of anger, selfish ambition, divisions, the feeling that everyone is wrong except those in your own little group, envy, drunkenness, wild parties, and other kinds of sin" popped up at the most awkward of times and some of these works continued to display themselves privately and publicly in my life.

You will find many believers flowing in the gifts of the Spirit but when you get close to them you are put may off by the lack of the fragrance of Christ in their character and nature. Paul wrote that it is God's desire that we be conformed to the image and likeness of His Son, Jesus Christ who operated 100 percent in all the fruits as well as the gifts of the Holy Spirit.

Let us not be content to walk in the gifts of the Spirit alone, but develop a balanced walk exhibiting both the fruit and the gifts of the Holy Spirit. Paul urges all believers to "work out our salvation with fear and trembling so that we become Christ like in our nature." This six week journey will open your heart and mind on how to cultivate and developing the various fruits in your life. Just as every natural fruit requires different attention and conditions for growth and harvesting, so also do the fruit of the Spirit. May you not be satisfied with where you are now but press on to be More like Jesus in your daily walk.

ACKNOWLEDGEMENTS

Do not withhold good from those who deserve it when it's in your power to help them.
Proverbs 3:2

A Call For Character by Greg Zoschak published by Harrison House ISBN 0-89274-893-1

Excerpts and Illustrations from www.sermoncentral.com

Thanks to Titi Kunkel for being my editor

Thanks to Elizabeth Banks at Data CPS for her wonderful gift and the ability to translate my thoughts into design work for the cover. She is truly a blessing.

Cover art by Ben Steed and courtesy of www.heartlight.org

A Heart of Love!

- Love is a choice.
- Love is a decision.
- You can only truly walk the love walk being hooked up to the One Who Is Love.
- Are you plugged in?

John Harvey wrote, "If you "Google" the word love, and you have to be very careful doing this, you will find all sorts of websites, 120,000,000 to be exact. Here are some examples that you will find: I love Dogs.com; I love Cats.com; I love Cheese. Com; I love Lucy.com; We love the Iraqi Information Minister.com; Matchmaker.com; The Love Calculator.com On this site you type in your name and your mates name and it gives you the odds of your relationship lasting. The interesting aspect is that on all these sites, love is seen as almost an entirely human endeavour."

The gift, without the giver, is bare.
CHARLES SHELDON

The Bible tells us that the fruit of the Spirit is love. (Gal 5:22) God is love, and that is where love originates. The quality of our love walk is dependent on the quality of our relationship with the author of love. You become like whom you hang around with. When we think of the fruit of love, we automatically think of cultivating and developing love relationships with others. Although this is important, the more important aspect of the fruit of love is to diligently cultivate and develop an individual love relationship with your Heavenly Father. The greatest commandment is not "Love one another", but as Jesus put it, "You must love the Lord your God with all your heart, all your soul, and all your mind.' This is the first and greatest commandment. A second is equally important: `Love your neighbour as yourself." (Matt 22:37-39) Most of us would feel quite comfortable in sitting down, conversing with and somehow expressing love to other members of the body of Christ. How would we act if Jesus was to walk into the room in the flesh to relax and converse with you?"

Apostle John wrote, "How can we be sure that we belong to him? By obeying his commandments. If someone says, "I belong to God," but doesn't obey God's commandments, that person is a liar and does not live in the truth. But those who obey God's word really do love him. That is the way to know whether or not we live in him. Those who say they live in God should live their lives as Christ did."

You will only be able to begin to walk in the love of God towards others when you have first learned and committed to love the Lord with all your heart, all your soul and all your mind. Love, according to God's definition is a tall order. Paul wrote, "Love never gives up. Love cares more for others than for self. Love doesn't want what it doesn't have. Love doesn't strut, Doesn't have a swelled head, doesn't force itself on others, Isn't always "me first," doesn't fly off the handle, Doesn't keep score of the sins of others, Doesn't revel when others grovel, Takes pleasure in the flowering of truth, Puts up with anything, Trusts God always, Always looks for the best, Never looks back, But keeps going to the end. Love never dies." (1 Cor 13:4-8 Msg) Just as we need to be plugged into the electric socket to let the electricity flow through, so also it is only the Love of God that powers our love walk. Are you plugged in to the Power of His Love today?

Prayer points:

- Father, a heart of love like Yours is my desire
- A heart full of grace, compassion, kindness, faith filled, forever true, strong as the wind, soft as the shadows.
- Lord, give me a heart like yours as I spend time plugged in, getting to know and love You with all my heart, soul and mind.

In Jesus' Name.
Amen

Verses for the Day:

"Follow God's example in everything you do, because you are his dear children. Live a life filled with love for others, following the example of Christ, who loved you and gave himself as a sacrifice to take away your sins. And God was pleased, because that sacrifice was like sweet perfume to him." (Eph 5:1-2)

Cultivating the Fruit of Love! (1)

- Being led by the Spirit is receiving instruction from God.
- Developing the character of Jesus is accomplished by developing the same fruits that were easily recognised in His life.
- It is by outward manifestation (fruit) that inward nature (character) is recognised.

Jesus said, "You shall know those who are His, by their fruits."(Matt 7:20) To develop faith in God, we first need to come to know Him. We do that by learning to cultivate the fruit of love towards Him. To know Him is to love Him. To love Him is to trust Him. To trust Him is to have faith in Him – the kind of faith which moves mountains. It is then that the heart receives its desires. There are three steps involved in cultivating the fruit of love towards the heavenly father. Today we will look at the first step.

Step one in the cultivation process is to develop sight of God. You need to sharpen your vision of the Father and thereby become more enlightened as to His personal attributes – who He is. Paul wrote, "Follow God's example in everything you do, because you are his dear children. Live a life filled with love for others, following the example of Christ, who loved you and gave himself as a sacrifice to take away your sins. And God was pleased, because that sacrifice was like sweet perfume to him." How did Jesus develop love in His life so that it produced one hundred fold? The secret is found in John 5:19. "Jesus replied, "I assure you, the Son can do nothing by himself. He does only what he sees the Father doing. Whatever the Father does, the Son also does." Unless you spend time with the Father you cannot walk in the God kind of love. The Bible tells us we cannot love without knowing God. (1 John 4:7-8) There are different levels of knowing God. Some just know about Him, some know Him but do not spend time with Him,

> **The Apostle Paul wrote, unless I have love, I am nothing.**
> **BILLY GRAHAM**

whereas others are always spending time with Him, listening to Him and doing His Will – which is His Word.

An example of Jesus overcoming temptation and evil with good by developing sight of God -separating Himself and spending time with the Father - was at the time of John the Baptist's death. In Matthew 14, the Bible tells us that King Herod placed John in prison for the sake of Herodias. After Herodias' daughter pleased Herod with her dancing, he swore to give her anything she asked for. After consulting her mother, she asked for and received the head of John the Baptist.

What would you have done? How would you have coped with this kind of situation? Could it be that Jesus was tempted not to walk in love? Being angry and wanting to retaliate would be the expected response of the flesh. According to Hebrews 4:15, "Jesus, was in all points tempted like as we are, yet was without sin." The Bible says, "As soon as Jesus heard the news, he went off by himself in a boat to a remote area to be alone. But the crowds heard where he was headed and followed by land from many villages. A vast crowd was there as he stepped from the boat, and he had compassion on them and healed their sick." (Matt 14:13-14) Following the death of John the Baptist, when He came into contact with people, He was moved with compassion – not bitterness or resentment – because the fruit of love had been cultivated and developed in His life through loving the Father.

May you cultivate the fruit of love today by spending time with the Father and developing sight of Him irrespective of all the situations and circumstances you face?

Prayer points:

- Father, thank You for showing me that the first way I need to cultivate the fruit of love is to spend time with You.
- May I catch sight of You and only do the things that I hear You speak to my heart to do.
- May I not react in the flesh to the situations, circumstances and people who come against me?
- May I truly walk like Jesus would walk, in love, today?

17

In Jesus' Name.
Amen

Verses for the Day:

"But Jesus replied, "My Father never stops working, so why should I?" So the Jewish leaders tried all the more to kill him. In addition to disobeying the Sabbath rules, he had spoken of God as his Father, thereby making himself equal with God. Jesus replied, "I assure you, the Son can do nothing by himself. He does only what he sees the Father doing. Whatever the Father does, the Son also does." (John 5:17-19)

Cultivating the Fruit of Love! (2)

- To walk in love you need to be hooked up to the agape love of the Father, who is love and the source of all love.
- If through the internet we can touch all parts of the world, easy to see how through the Spirit we can be connected to the Power of His Love.
- How do we develop our love walk with the Father?

The second step of the developing process of our love relationship with our heavenly Father is to pray in the Spirit. Jude wrote, "But ye, beloved, building up yourselves on your most holy faith, praying in the Holy Ghost, keep yourselves in the love of God, looking for the mercy of our Lord Jesus Christ unto eternal life." (Jude 20, 21) According to this passage, praying in the Holy Ghost keeps the love of God stirred up and cultivates it. It is so easy to lose focus when you are surrounded with situations, troubles and life issues on every side.

When love is suppressed, hate takes its place.
HAVELOCK ELLIS

In John 21, on three occasions Jesus asked Peter if he loved Him. We all wonder why Jesus had to repeat the same question three times. On the first two occasions when Jesus asked, "Do you love me?" He used the Greek word 'agape' for love, meaning unconditional love. This God-kind of love is the type of love that will continue to love people regardless of whether or not it receives a response. The reason Jesus repeated His question was because on the three occasions Peter answered; "I love you", using the Greek word 'phileo' for love, meaning conditional love. This kind of love is the one that changes according to the response it receives. On the final occasion Jesus changed his love from 'agape' to 'phileo' to acknowledge that Peter had not reached that higher level of unconditional love of the Father or Him. Peter was in need of cultivating his love relationship with his Lord.

In 1 Peter 1:7-8, Peter expressed a relationship of 'agape' love with Jesus that he could not express in John 21. Something had taken place after Peter had been filled with the Holy Ghost on the day of Pentecost. "On the day of Pentecost, seven weeks after Jesus' resurrections, the believers were meeting together in one place. Suddenly there was a sound from heaven like the roaring of a mighty windstorm in the skies about them, and it filled the house where they were meeting. Then, what looked like flames or tongues of fire appeared and settled on each of them. And everyone present was filled with the Holy Spirit and began speaking in other tongues, as the Holy Spirit gave them this ability.(Acts 2:4) His love for the Lord had greatly increased and the experience of the infilling of the Holy Ghost had brought him into a closer love walk with the Father.

The Bible tells us in Romans 8:29 that the "Holy Spirit helps us in our distress. For we don't know what we should pray for, nor how we should pray. But the Holy Spirit prays for us with groanings that cannot be expressed in words." We all need the infilling or baptism of the Holy Spirit to help us develop our love relationship with God.

Develop your love relationship with the Lord and with the Father today. Build yourself up in your most Holy Faith, praying in the Spirit.

Prayer points:

- Father, thank your for showing me how to develop my love relationship with You.
- I receive the infilling of Your Holy Spirit which is a gift from You.
- May I develop my heavenly prayer language through which I draw closer to You and enter into a deeper love relationship with You?
- Bring people around me who will help me walk in a deeper relationship with You.

In Jesus' Name.
Amen

Verse for the Day:

"And they were all filled with the Holy Ghost, and began to speak with other tongues, as the Spirit gave them utterance." (Acts 2:4)

Day 4

Cultivating the Fruit of Love! (3)

- To develop the fruit of love, one has to practice love.
- Feelings follow actions.
- True feelings associated with love will never come apart from the Father, for He is love.

Apostle John wrote, "No one has ever seen God. But if we love each other, God lives in us, and his love has been brought to full expression through us." (1 John 4:12) God's love is perfected in believers who choose to love each other. What kind of love was John talking about? He must have definitely been referring to the 'agape' or unconditional love that God has for each one of His creation.

The main hindrance to showing love one to another is the tendency to wait for a feeling prior to taking some type of action that would somehow express love. But love is not a feeling. Since God is love and God is the Word, (John 1:1), then love is putting the Word of God into practice. If we do that, we will be cultivating the fruit of love in our lives.

> **Give people not only your care, but your heart.**
> **MOTHER TERESA**

There are many who want to cultivate their relationship with the Father, so they begin praying in the Spirit for a short time. They complain they don't feel anything so they stop praying. If you are persistent, however, and continue diligently to cultivate the fruit of love towards the Father, then the feeling of love would eventually come.

The Bible says if someone has wronged you and you have unforgiveness towards them, "go and tell him/her his fault between you and him/her alone: if he/she shall hear thee, then you will gain a brother/sister." (Matt 18:15) Many times we either do not do the Word of God, or when we do, we think it is our responsibility to ensure the person is convicted of their wrong and ensure that they have repented. Many times we fail to accept an apology for what it is, feeling that the apology from the mouth is not enough and start judging the attitude of their hearts, which God alone can judge. Paul urged the Ephesians, "Instead, be kind to each other, tender hearted, forgiving one another, just as God through Christ has forgiven you." (Eph 4:32)

The God kind of love defined by Paul in 1 Cor 13:4-7 is the type that "endures long and is patient and kind; the kind of love that never is envious nor boils over with jealousy. This love is not boastful or vainglorious, and does not display itself haughtily. This kind of love is not conceited (arrogant and inflated with pride). It is not rude (unmannerly) and does not act unbecomingly. Love (God's love in us) does not insist on its own rights or its own way, for it is not self-seeking; it is not touchy or fretful or resentful; it takes no account of the evil done to it [it pays no attention to a suffered wrong]. It does not rejoice at injustice and unrighteousness, but rejoices when right and truth prevail. The kind of love that bears up under anything and everything that comes, is ever ready to believe the best of every person, its hopes are fadeless under all circumstances, and it endures everything [without weakening]. This God kind of love never fails [never fades out or becomes obsolete or comes to an end].

May we walk in godly love towards our Heavenly Father and His Word and towards others, today?

Prayer points:

- Father, thank You for Your Word that is a light to our path and a lamp to our feet.
- Help us to walk according to Your Word today.
- May I begin the process of cultivation of love so I may truly love You with all my heart, my soul and all my mind?
- That is, after all the first and great commandment.

In Jesus' Name.
Amen

<u>Verse for the Day</u>:

"Jesus said, "Love the Lord your God with all your passion and prayer and intelligence." (Matt 22:37 Msg)

Day 5

Showing You Care!

"And let us consider how we may spur one another on toward love and good deeds." (Heb 10:24)

- To love and be loved…what could be more important?
- Did you know that people express and receive love in different ways?
- Find out the love language of those around you by listening to what they complain about.

At a Bible Study last week in Cambridge, I asked how they knew when someone cared about them. They all gave different responses. Here were some of the replies:

- Spending time with them.
- Understanding the situations they were in.
- Acts of kindness
- A listening ear
- Giving of gifts.

Dr Gary Chapman has found that throughout his counselling, truly connecting with a person or more importantly a loved one came down to one simple fact: you need to know and speak his or her love language. A love language is the way we express our devotion and commitment, and it can be learned or changed to touch the hearts of those around us. Whether you're a friend, a spouse, a parent, a work colleague or a single, the five love languages are the same.

Below are the different love languages people speak and examples of each of them.

1. Words of Affirmation–
2. Receiving Gifts
3. Quality Time
4. Acts of Service
5. Physical Touch

I have a husband, three sons and a daughter and they all speak different love languages. My daughter's love languages are receiving gifts and spending quality time with her friends and family. My husband and sons are all quite different and to help them feel loved, I need to communicate my love to them in different ways to speak to them individually.

Through my own experience I have found that you may sincerely love someone but find that if you are expressing your love to them in a language that they do not understand they may still feel unloved. You hear about the lady who says, "My husband never buys me flowers", although her husband makes sure he provides everything he feels she needs in the house. His love language may be acts of service, whereas hers may be the receiving of gifts. You may have a lady who buys gifts for everyone and finds that some of the recipients would have rather appreciated a word of affirmation or just a hug or an arm around their neck.

It is so important that we make the effort to love one another the way the Lord prayed for us to. May we take the time to find out the love languages that those around us speak so we can show them in a way they can understand, that we care for them.

Prayer Points:

- Heavenly Father, thank You for opening my eyes to the many ways we can express and receive love.
- Help me to understand the things that people do to me that communicate their love to me.
- Help me to understand how I can best communicate love to those close to me.
- May I walk in love towards those around me today?

In Jesus' Name I pray,
Amen

Joy: the Power to Overcome (1)

- The definition of joy.
- Difference between happiness and joy
- Why you need joy.

The Webster Dictionary defines 'joy' as intense happiness or great delight; the outward expression of emotion. The Word of God identifies joy as one of the nine fruit of the Spirit in Galatians 5:22-23. This joy comes by the Spirit of God and is not the same as what the world refers to as 'happiness'. Happiness depends largely upon happenings, such as feeling good, close friendships and pleasant surroundings whereas joy bubbles up from within as a result of being rightly related to God and having His Spirit living big on the inside of you.

Moses told the chosen children of Israel, "Because you didn't serve GOD, your God, out of the joy and goodness of your heart in the great abundance, you'll have to serve your enemies. Life will be famine and drought, rags and wretchedness; then he'll put an iron yoke on your neck until he's destroyed you. (Deut 28:47, 48) These scriptures reveal the consequences of serving God without joy. According to this, the absence of joy in believers' lives results in them serving the enemy, wanting all things, and having a yoke of iron placed upon their necks. On the other hand, for those who serve the Lord with joy and with gladness of heart, the opposite will be true. They will overcome the enemy and experience fulfilment in all things and be free of the yoke of bondage. The fruit of joy fulfils three functions:

There is no cosmetic for beauty like a joyful spirit.
MARGUERITE, COUNTESS OF BLESSINGTON

- To produce victory
- To provide fulfilment
- To protect from oppression.

Whatever overcomes you becomes your master. During times of trial we can assess the degree to which we are in bondage to the enemy by measuring the extent to which our trials overcome us. How do you respond when you suffer through an extended illness? How do you react when the enemy sits up your family or friends to persistently harass and persecute you? How do you bear up under lengthy trials as opposed to brief ones? How am I honestly conducting myself in the midst of the trials which I am experiencing right now? Peter wrote, "For you are a slave to whatever controls you." (2 Peter 2:19)

It takes effort to cultivate and develop the fruit of joy in your life. Joy begins on the inside of a person and is not dependent on outward circumstances. Joy is the strength that enables you to remain, "strong and steady, always enthusiastic about the Lord's work, for you know that nothing you do for the Lord is ever useless." (1 Cor 15:58)

Joy is a preventative fruit that protects against falling into bondage and servitude to the enemy of God. God wants you to rejoice even in times of trial. Peter wrote, "Friends, when life gets really difficult, don't jump to the conclusion that God isn't on the job. Instead, be glad that you are in the very thick of what Christ experienced. This is a spiritual refining process, with glory just around the corner." (1 Peter 4:12-13) Since your flesh does not want to do this, the only way you can do this is through the development of the fruit of Joy, by the power of the Holy Spirit in your life. Determine in your heart today that no one is going to steal your joy that Jesus gives you because He loves you. That you are going to walk in victory by maintaining an attitude of joy in the Lord.

Prayer points:

- Father, thank You for the Holy Spirit on the inside of me who enables and helps me to develop the fruit of joy in my life.
- Help me to rejoice in the knowledge that greater are You who live on the inside of me, than he that is in the world.
- Thank You that the same Spirit that raised Christ from the dead dwells in me.

- May I allow the fruit of joy to grow in my life today as I yield to the Holy Spirit within me to face the hard, unpleasant challenges and trials of the day.

In Jesus' Name.
Amen

<u>Verse for the Day</u>:

"You will show me the path of life; in Your presence is fullness of joy, at Your right hand there are pleasures forevermore." (Psalm 16:11)

Joy: Lost Yours? (2)

- Why many people have lost their song
- God can restore your joy.
- Promise of the supply of joy.

Many believers have lost their joy and do not want to admit that it has happened. They walk around like a bear with a sore head or look like they have been sucking on a lemon. Why have so many people lost their song? Why has the flow stopped? Why the blockage? A few reasons are sin and disobedience to God; un forgiveness, pride, strife, bitterness, resentment and lack of repentance. The Christian who has lost his/her joy is a pitiful sight.

No matter what has caused you to lose your joy, King David showed us that joy can be restored. He wrote, "Restore to me again the joy of your salvation, and make me willing to obey you." (Psalms 51:12) He did not ask God to return his salvation, for he never lost it, but rather his request is for joy.

A merry heart doeth good like a medicine.
PROVERBS 17:22

The word "restore" implies that it is something that the Psalmist once had and needed to recover. To "restore" can mean "to bring back into a normal or former condition." When one restores an old car, building or painting, it means the owner seeks to bring the item back as close as is possible, to what it was when it was new.

The reason for David's loss of joy was because sin and disobedience had run its course in his life through his sin with Bathsheba, who was the wife of Uriah the Hittite. Rebellion, adultery and murder had caused tremendous problems. He found that sin had hardened his heart, hindered his progress and caused him to lose his joy. Unconfessed sin results in a loss of joy, because it grieves the Holy Ghost, who produces joy in the heart of every believer. Sin handicaps a believer. It so cripples one's life that he or she cannot think right, walk right, or feel right. he had lost his joy was because of his sin.

30

When confronted by Prophet Nathan about his sin, we see a repentant attitude, an acknowledgement of God's goodness and mercy, and a confession of sin by David.

"Have mercy on me, O God, because of your unfailing love. Because of your great compassion, blot out the stain of my sins. Wash me clean from my guilt. Purify me from my sin. For I recognize my shameful deeds--they haunt me day and night. Against you, and you alone, have I sinned; I have done what is evil in your sight. You will be proved right in what you say, and your judgment against me is just. For I was born a sinner--yes, from the moment my mother conceived me. But you desire honesty from the heart, so you can teach me to be wise in my inmost being." (Psalm 51:1-6)

The restoration of his joy began with his request. No one ever recovers lost joy until there is a request for its return. Notice a few things about David's request. It was earnest, expectant, expressive and honest.

There are two major results of restoration in David's life. "Then I will teach your ways to sinners, and they will return to you." (Psalm 51:13) The restoration of joy in his life caused him to teach people the ways of God and sinners, as a result, getting saved.

Have you experienced the joy of Salvation? Have you lost the joy of your Salvation? If you answered yes to either of these questions let me say that joy can be received through Jesus Christ, and joy can be restored through Him as well.

Prayer points:

- Father, thank You for opening my eyes to see that joy is part of my inheritance as Your child.
- Thank You for showing me what has caused me to lose my joy.
- Father, restore to me the joy of my salvation.
- May my joy be full as I dwell in Your Word and Presence.

- Thank You for reminding me that no one can take away the joy that You place in my heart because You died for me, paid for my total redemption, believe in me and love me.

In Jesus' Name.
Amen

Verses for the Day:

"Even though the fig trees have no blossoms, and there are no grapes on the vine; even though the olive crop fails, and the fields lie empty and barren; even though the flocks die in the fields, and the cattle barns are empty, yet I will rejoice in the LORD! I will be joyful in the God of my salvation. The Sovereign LORD is my strength! He will make me as surefooted as a deer and bring me safely over the mountains." (Habakkuk 3:17-19)

Joy: How It Grows! (3)

- How do we cultivate the fruit of joy in our lives

There are three ways of cultivating the fruit of joy in our lives.

- By developing our faith.
- By giving of ourselves to others.
- By seeking God's presence

Although we know that faith comes by hearing the Word of God, (Rom 10:17) many do not know of the close relationship between joy, faith and the Word. Jesus told His disciples after speaking the Word to them, "I have told you this so that you will be filled with my joy. Yes, your joy will overflow!" David in Psalm 19:8 recorded the truth of joy coming from the Word of God: "The commandments of the LORD are right, bringing joy to the heart." Prophet Jeremiah wrote, "Your words are what sustain me. They bring me great joy and are my heart's delight, for I bear your name, O LORD God Almighty." (Jer 15:16) Just as there is no faith outside the Word of God, likewise there is no faith outside of joy; and there is no joy outside of faith. Faith and joy stand together upon the solid foundation of the eternal Word of God. Those with weak faith and little joy spend a limited amount of quality time in God's Word. They are not able to 'count it all joy' during their trials because they do not have the solid faith that, come what may, God will provide for their needs. As long as you live in the realm of doubt and unbelief, you will never experience joy. Paul wrote in Rom 15:13, "So I pray that God, who gives you hope, will keep you happy and full of peace as you believe in him."

> **Those who sow in tears will reap with songs of joy.**
> **PSALM 126:5**

The second way of cultivating joy is by giving yourself to others. Many believers don't have joy simply because they are self-centred, and yet self-centredness is the natural tendency of the flesh for those who are going through trials. If we would learn to reach out to other and minister to someone else during our times of trial we could turn our self pity into joy by a simple act of the will: "And the Lord turned the captivity of Job, when he prayed for his friends" (Job 42:10). "He that goes forth with weeping, bearing precious seed, shall doubtless come again with rejoicing bringing the sheaves with him. (Ps 126:6)

Thirdly, we cultivate joy by seeking God's presence. The three basic elements of how to seek God's presence is found in James 4:8: "Draw close to God, and God will draw close to you. Wash your hands, you sinners; purify your hearts, you hypocrites." The first way is to draw near to God simply by an act of your will. We must take the initiative and pay the price of seeking it. God is not selective about those who draw near to Him. It is up to us individually. Secondly, to seek God's presence is to cleanse the hands. Trying to seek God's presence with un confessed sin in your life will prove to be frustrating because Isaiah 59:2 says God hides His face from sin or iniquity. Jesus made it easy for us to cleanse ourselves before seeking God's presence. All we need to do its to ask for forgiveness and repent of our sin. (1 John 1:9) He promises to forgive us and cleanse us from all unrighteousness. Thirdly we need to purify our hearts. We must not be double-minded but seek God with our whole heart. We must give Him undivided attention.

God wants you to cultivate and develop the fruit of joy so that you will be an over comer and a great witness to those in the world. Many, through you, will "taste and see that the Lord is good." (Ps 34:8)

Prayer points:

- Father, thank You for showing me how to cultivate the fruit of joy in my life.
- May I develop my faith as through that I will be more joyful.
- Help me to give myself to others in service and through that see my joy fulfilled.
- May I seek Your presence, for in Your presence is fullness of joy.

- May my life be filled with joy, so that others may taste and see that the Lord is good.

In Jesus' Name.
Amen

Verse for the Day:

"I have told you this so that you will be filled with my joy. Yes, your joy will overflow!" (John 15:11)

Joy: Principles of Joy! (4)

- One of the great characteristics of the Christian is the joy that we have.
- Joy is tuning in to what God is doing around you.
- Joy is seeing the world through God's eyes.

To the Jewish people wine symbolized joy. The Jewish rabbis had a saying, 'Without wine there is no joy." At the wedding in Cana their joy had run out! This statement by the mother of Jesus goes beyond liquid refreshment at a wedding. It is symbolic of our lives. It is a reminder of the emptiness of our life without Christ. It is a scary thing when the "wine runs out."

Ernest Hemmingway was a famous writer, but you might not know many details about his life. Hemmingway was a great storyteller. Many of his books are considered to be classics. The Old Man and The Sea, a story he wrote while living in Cuba reveal his genius. He was a Nobel Prize recipient. From the very early years of his life he was a person who went for it all. He was a newspaper reporter and an ambulance driver during WWI. He was involved in the Spanish Civil War. He had friendships that ranged from bullfighters to authors. Whatever he did, he went for it all, he was drinking long at the natural wine of life. But there came a day when those wines ran out. Carlos Baker records in the biography of Hemmingway that one bright, cloudless Sunday morning, Ernest shot and killed himself. There are times when the wine runs out. The joy is dry!

Rejoice in the Lord always. I will say it again, rejoice.
PHILIPPIANS 4:4

Billy Graham said in his message "Saved or Lost" in Texas in 1965. "..one of the fruits of the Spirit is joy. You might not be able to work up joy yourself, but God the Holy Spirit living inside of you can produce this joy supernaturally, and a Christian is to have joy. He went on to say, "A Christian is to have joy. That's one of the great characteristics of the Christian is the joy that we have, and if you don't have this joy and if you don't have this peace that Christ gives, you had better search your heart and find out if you really know Christ."

Someone wrote, "Joy is like the hidden note in the glass. Joy is tuning in to what God is doing around you, seeing the world through his eyes, picking up on his delight in us as his children. Anyone can find happiness for a while… Happiness depends on what is happening to you. Joy is different; joy goes deeper. Joy is when your whole being sings because you have caught a glimpse of God at work. Joy can creep up on you and surprise you in unexpected places."

Joy begins on the inside and is not dependent on outward circumstance. Here are seven principles of Joy:

- In God's presence is fullness of joy – Psalm 16:11
- If we abide in the Lord, our joy will be full – John 15:7-11
- Another human being cannot take your joy from you – John 16:22
- Answered prayer brings full joy – John 16:23-24
- The joy of the Lord is our strength – Nehemiah 8:10
- God commands joy – Psalm 100:2; Philippians 4:4
- Joy is like a medicine – Proverbs 17:22

May you drink in the wine of joy that Christ brings to you by the power of the Holy Spirit today.

Prayer points:

- Father, thank You that the Holy Spirit living on the inside of me produces the fruit of the Spirit is joy.
- Help me to cooperate with the Spirit of God, that my joy may be full.
- May I spend time in Your presence today to soak in the joy of knowing and loving You.
- May You fill me with the joy of my salvation, great inheritance and future.
- May this joy spill over onto all those around me.

In Jesus' Name.
Amen

Verse for the Day·

"And Nehemiah continued, "Go and celebrate with a feast of choice
foods and sweet drinks, and share gifts of food with people who
have nothing prepared. This is a sacred day before our Lord. Don't
be dejected and sad, for the joy of the LORD is your strength!" (Neh
8:10)

Peace: A Troubled Heart? (1)

- But the fruit of the spirit is …peace.
- The fruit of peace is to prevent the hearts of God's people from being troubled.
- God blesses those who work for peace, for they will be called the children of God.

The first function of the fruit of peace is to prevent the hearts of God's people from being troubled.

Jesus told his disciples, "Don't let anyone mislead you. For many will come in my name, saying, `I am the Messiah.' They will lead many astray. And wars will break out near and far, but don't panic. Yes, these things must come, but the end won't follow immediately. The nations and kingdoms will proclaim war against each other, and there will be famines and earthquakes in many parts of the world. But all this will be only the beginning of the horrors to come." He was telling them that just as He had to go to the cross, there will be some things that will come on earth and around your life that you cannot pray, fast or confess away. Jesus explained this and told His disciples not 'to panic or be troubled'.

> **Because the Lord is my Shepherd, I have everything I need.**
> **PSALM 23:1 TLB**

The presence of peace is the thing that will keep trouble out of your heart. Before He left the earth, Jesus gave us this parting word: "I am leaving you with a gift--peace of mind and heart. And the peace I give isn't like the peace the world gives. So don't be troubled or afraid." Although Jesus gave us His peace, God is not going to come down and automatically establish peace in your heart. We must take the initiative and individually cultivate the fruit of peace in our own hearts.

Isaiah gave insight on how to maintain an attitude of peace. "You will keep in perfect peace all who trust in you, whose thoughts are fixed on you! (Is 26:3)

To maintain an attitude of peace by the Spirit of God is our only means of preservation. Paul wrote, "Don't worry about anything; instead, pray about everything. Tell God what you need, and thank him for all he has done. If you do this, you will experience God's peace, which is far more wonderful than the human mind can understand. His peace will guard your hearts and minds as you live in Christ Jesus." (Phil 4:6-7)

We have to guard our heart and mind against the enemy and not let down our guard. The reason why many believers are overcome by the numerous attacks of the enemy in these troublesome times is because they have let down their guard. The story of Mary and Martha contrasts the troubled believer with the believer who is at peace. (Luke 10:38-42) When a believer is troubled the following happens: they firstly neglect the most needful part of their life – which is to sit at the feet of Jesus and hear His Word. Secondly many times believers try to substitute serving the Lord for sitting at His feet.

There once was a King who offered a prize to the artist who would paint the best picture of peace. Many artists tried. The King looked at all the pictures, but there were only two he really liked and he had to choose between them. One picture was of a calm lake. The lake was a perfect mirror for peaceful towering mountains were all around it. Overhead was a blue sky with fluffy white clouds. All who saw this picture thought that it was a perfect picture of peace. The other picture had mountains too. But these were rugged and bare. Above was an angry sky from which rain fell, in which lightening played. Down the side of the mountain tumbled a foaming waterfall. This did not look peaceful at all. But when the King looked, he saw behind the waterfall a tiny bush growing in a crack in the rock. In the bush a mother bird had built her nest. There, in the midst of the rush of angry water, sat the mother bird on her nest .... perfect peace. Which picture do you think won the prize? The King chose the second picture. Do you know why? "Because," explained the King, "peace does not mean to be in a place where there is no noise, trouble, or hard work. Peace means to be in the midst of all those things and still be calm in your heart. That is the real meaning of peace."

Today, may your decision be to trust in the Lord and fix your thoughts on Him. May you find the time to sit at His feet and hear His Words of Peace to you.

Prayer points:

- Father, thank You for showing me that You paid the price for my peace.
- That You are the Prince of Peace and Your Gospel is a gospel of Peace.
- That peace comes to me as I trust and obey Your Words to me.
- May I walk in Your peace that passes all human understanding as I trust in You.

In Jesus' Name.
Amen

Verses for the Day:

"Do not fret or have any anxiety about anything, but in every circumstance and in everything, by prayer and petition (definite requests), with thanksgiving, continue to make your wants known to God. And God's peace [shall be yours, that tranquil state of a soul assured of its salvation through Christ, and so fearing nothing from God and being content with its earthly lot of whatever sort that is, that peace] which transcends all understanding shall garrison and mount guard over your hearts and minds in Christ Jesus." (Phil 4:6-7 Amp)

Peace: Determine Your Direction! (2)

* The fruit of peace is to determine direction.
* The green light of peace in your heart means go, and the red light means stop.
* God's peace protects and directs His people in His perfect will.

God uses the fruit of peace to guide our steps so that our lives will be in keeping with His perfect plan and purpose. Paul wrote to the Colossian Christians, "And let the peace that comes from Christ rule in your hearts. For as members of one body you are all called to live in peace. And always be thankful." (Col 3:15)

Once again it is your responsibility to 'let' peace rule in your heart. Peace has to be developed as an act of your will and through practice. The word 'rule' in the Greek means "to act as an umpire.., to arbitrate, decide. In other words the peace of God will be a deciding factor in a believer's heart.

God uses the fruit of peace to guide our steps so that our lives will be in keeping with His perfect plan and purpose. If you need to make a decision about moving locations, moving jobs, getting married, buying this particular item or another, opening up this or that business, by cultivating the fruit of peace in your life, this will guide you concerning whether, when, where, and how to make the move. A Christian should not take any steps until they experience a strong peace about each step that is involved. If you wait on the peace of God, you will discover that every detail of the move will fall into place beautifully.

A heart at peace gives life to the body.
PROVERBS 14:30

Many of us are tempted to jumping ahead of God and going on without His peace. We must learn to listen to our heart and detect whether or not we are peaceful or disturbed concerning the decision that is about to be made. As we become sensitive to the leading of God's peace, we will become better able to perceive the leading of

His Spirit. Learning to walk in God's peace is a process and until we learn to get it right we can be discouraged when we miss it. Continued effort will result in eventual success. "And let us not be weary in well doing: for in due season we shall reap, if we faint not." (Gal 6:9)

As you cultivate the fruit of peace, it will keep you safe within the boundaries of God's will. Just as an umpire blows the whistle when a player steps out of bounds, so will the peace of God lift when you step out of God's will for your life? God will use the fruit of peace to keep His children within the boundaries of His divine protection. "The thief's purpose is to steal and kill and destroy. My purpose is to give life in all its fullness." (John 10:10)

Today, may you be sensitive to the leading of the Holy Spirit by the fruit of peace in your heart.

Prayer points:

- Father, thank You for revelation of the purpose of the fruit of peace in our lives.
- Help me to cultivate and develop Your peace in my heart.
- May I learn to follow the leading of Your peace in my heart today.

In Jesus' Name.
Amen

Verse for the Day:

"May grace (God's unmerited favour) and spiritual peace [which means peace with God and harmony, unity, and undisturbed ness] be yours from God our Father and from the Lord Jesus Christ.." (Eph 1:2)

Peace: Are You A Peacemaker? (3)

- God blesses those who work for peace, for they will be called the children of God.
- We must pursue peaceful ends, by peaceful means.

A function of the fruit of peace is to enable believers to be peacemakers. Wise King Solomon counselled us: "Keep your heart with all diligence; for out of it are the issues of life." (Prov 4:23) Whatever is in the hearts of people will be manifested in their treatment of one another. Believers who are irritable, rude and moody in their actions toward others are that way because that is what is in their heart. We can only give to others what we possess ourselves.

Jesus is a perfect example of a heart filled with peace. One of his names is the Prince of Peace (Is 9:6) which enabled him to minister grace, mercy, love and peace to all those with whom He came in contact.

For He Himself is our peace.

EPHESIANS 2:14

One characteristic of peacemakers is their non-resistance in the natural realm to evil that comes against them by others. Too many Christians are always concerned that they obtain their rights, express their opinions, and take whatever actions they feel are justified in every situation that arises against them. Jesus Christ's gospel no longer promoted 'an eye for an eye and a tooth for a tooth mentality, but rather it is a kind word for malicious slander or a charitable response for an evil action. (Matt 5:10-12) Paul wrote, "We are human, but we don't wage war with human plans and methods. We use God's mighty weapons, not mere worldly weapons, to knock down the Devil's strongholds. With these weapons we break down every proud argument that keeps people from knowing God. With these weapons we conquer their rebellious ideas, and we teach them to obey Christ. And we will punish those who remained disobedient after the rest of you became loyal and obedient. (2 Cor 10:3-6)

Paul urged the Christians, "Dear friends, never avenge yourselves. Leave that to God. For it is written," I will take vengeance; I will repay those who deserve it," says the Lord. Instead, do what the Scriptures say: "If your enemies are hungry, feed them. If they are thirsty, give them something to drink, and they will be ashamed of what they have done to you." Don't let evil get the best of you, but conquer evil by doing good." (Rom 12:19-21) Do not try and play God by taking your own revenge and ending up in a dangerous snare.

Jesus gave this counsel, "But I say, love your enemies! Pray for those who persecute you! In that way, you will be acting as true children of your Father in heaven. For he gives his sunlight to both the evil and the good, and he sends rain on the just and on the unjust, too." (Matt 5:44-45)

Only as you cultivate and develop the fruit of peace will you have the strength to bestow love, blessings, kindnesses and prayers upon those who either outwardly or subtly resist us with evil. Obeying this particular teaching of Jesus will make us over comers so that we may be true children of our Father in heaven. It is for this reason that the peacemakers are blessed, because they are the children of God.

Prayer points:

- Father, thank You for showing me how to act in the face of evil acts towards me.
- Help me to resist taking matters into my own hands and seeking revenge.
- Help me to guard my heart and allow only Your words and will to guide me.

In Jesus' Name.
Amen

Verses for the Day:

"Dear friends, never avenge yourselves. Leave that to God. For it is written," I will take vengeance; I will repay those who deserve it," says the Lord. Instead, do what the Scriptures say: "If your enemies are hungry, feed them. If they are thirsty, give them something to drink, and they will be ashamed of what they have done to you."

Don't let evil get the best of you, but conquer evil by doing good."
(Rom 12:19-21)

Peace: Cultivating It in Your Life! (4)

- Prayer produces the peace of God.
- Abiding in Jesus is the second way in which you may cultivate the fruit of peace in your life.
- Great peace have they which love thy law: and nothing shall offend them.

If you have ever known the lack of peace in your life then you will value the peace of God that passes all human understanding. There was a period in my life when although a Christian I literally felt I will living in hell because of all that was happening in and around me. My prayer for the peace of God in my life came as I submitted to the Word and Will of God for my life.

Here are three ways of cultivating and developing the fruit of peace in your life:

Prayer produces the peace of God. Paul wrote, "Don't worry about anything; instead, pray about everything. Tell God what you need, and thank him for all he has done. If you do this, you will experience God's peace, which is far more wonderful than the human mind can understand. His peace will guard your hearts and minds as you live in Christ Jesus. (Phil 4:6-7)

If it is possible, as far as it depends on you, live at peace with everyone.
ROMANS 12:18

Many Christians pray about their situations but are still troubled when they rise from their knees. The reason being that they neglect the thanksgiving which is the expressions of appreciation that God has heard and answered in the prayer just offered. It takes faith to give thanks when you have not seen the physical manifestation of what you have prayed for. Prayer and petition alone will not bring peace to the heart. A thankful heart will. It is only then that the peace of God will guard the heart and mind as thought they were encircled by a military garrison. God honours faith. (Heb 11:6)

Abiding in Jesus is the second way in which you may cultivate the fruit of peace in your life. "Remain in me, and I will remain in you. For a branch cannot produce fruit if it is severed from the vine, and you cannot be fruitful apart from me. "Yes, I am the vine; you are the branches. Those who remain in me, and I in them, will produce much fruit. For apart from me you can do nothing." (John 15:4-5) The fruit of peace will be developed in our lives as we remain in Jesus. We find the freedom to live when we die to self because peace and security in Jesus come only when self has been dethroned and Christ installed in its place.

Loving the Word of the Lord is the third way in which we cultivate peace in our lives. David wrote, "Great peace have they which love thy law: and nothing shall offend them." (Ps 119:165) In John 14:21 Jesus gave us an indicator by which we can measure the degree of our love for Him: "Those who obey my commandments are the ones who love me. And because they love me, my Father will love them, and I will love them. And I will reveal myself to each one of them."

The world has a type of peace to offer which is unstable, short-lived, and a doomed substitute for true lasting peace. Jesus said, "I am leaving you with a gift--peace of mind and heart. And the peace I give isn't like the peace the world gives. So don't be troubled or afraid." (John 14:27)

As a child of God you are promised peace in your house, peace in the land, peace in the grave, peace in prosperity, peace in your mind, peace in your soul, peace in your heart, peace in abundance, peace throughout eternity. The child of God lives in peace, lies down in peace, sleeps in peace, sows in peace, follows peace, comes in peace, departs in peace, seeks peace and preaches peace. He experiences perfect peace, great peace, multiplied peace, peace within, peace with his enemies, peace beyond understanding and peace with God, all made possible by the Prince of Peace! "But he was wounded and crushed for our sins. He was beaten that we might have peace. He was whipped, and we were healed!" (Is 53:5) Jesus IS your peace today and everyday!

Prayer points:

- Father, thank You that Jesus paid the price for my peace at Calvary.
- Thank You for the good news of peace that He brings to all who believe in Him.
- May I cultivate the fruit of peace in my life through prayer, abiding and remaining in His Word and giving His Word first priority and highest authority within my life.
- Thank You for the peace of God that passes all understanding.

In Jesus' Name.
Amen

Verse for the Day:

"And the peace of God, which surpasses all understanding, will guard your hearts and minds through Christ Jesus." (Phil 4:7)

Patience: Standing Up Under Pressure! (1)

- He that shall endure to the end shall be saved.
- By standing firm, you will win your souls.
- Endurance is "the capacity to remain firm under suffering without yielding to anger, resentment, despair or self pity.

"But the fruit of the Spirit is patience. (Gal 5:22) The word 'patience' in the Greek is translated 'longsuffering' which means "to suffer long, to gird up under pressure, persecution, distress, and trouble; to remain steadfast; patience.

Many Christians are trying to be led by the Spirit of God without being willing to suffer in the flesh, their lives are silently witnessing to the world that being a Christian is great – as long as things are going well. How do you behave when things begin to go wrong? What are your attitudes and actions like? It is through these times of personal suffering that you are often the most effective witness to the world. It is then that unbelievers can best see the difference that knowing the Lord makes in the life of an individual.

The first function of the fruit of longsuffering or patience is to produce endurance. Endurance is "the capacity to remain firm under suffering without yielding to anger, resentment, despair or self pity." In Hebrews we see that God has called us to run our race with patient endurance. "Therefore, since we are surrounded by such a huge crowd of witnesses to the life of faith, let us strip off every weight that slows us down, especially the sin that so easily hinders our progress.

> **Patience is not passive; on the contrary it is active; it is concentrated strength.**
> **EDWARD BULWER**

And let us run with endurance the race that God has set before us." (Heb 12:1) Our race is not a short sprint requiring great speed. It is a long gruelling type of race requiring endurance.

Paul is a perfect example of how to run the Christian race with endurance. He testified of what he was called to endure in order to finding the course set before him. He wrote:

"They say they serve Christ? I know I sound like a madman, but I have served him far more! I have worked harder, been put in jail more often, been whipped times without number, and faced death again and again. Five different times the Jews gave me thirty-nine lashes. Three times I was beaten with rods. Once I was stoned. Three times I was shipwrecked. Once I spent a whole night and a day adrift at sea. I have travelled many weary miles. I have faced danger from flooded rivers and from robbers. I have faced danger from my own people, the Jews, as well as from the Gentiles. I have faced danger in the cities, in the deserts, and on the stormy seas. And I have faced danger from men who claim to be Christians but are not. I have lived with weariness and pain and sleepless nights. Often I have been hungry and thirsty and have gone without food. Often I have shivered with cold, without enough clothing to keep me warm. Then, besides all this, I have the daily burden of how the churches are getting along." 2 Cor 11:23-28

Paul continued to persevere in the face of suffering and oppression because he saw past the hardships of the race to the prise which awaited him at the finish line. He allowed nothing to deter him from reaching the goal and reward which lay ahead.

"Jesus, the author and finisher of our faith; who for the joy that was set before him endured the cross, despising the shame, and is now set down at the right hand of the throne of God." (Heb 12:2) For this reason, you must develop the fruit of longsuffering or patience today if you hope to fight the good fight of faith and run the race set before you.

Prayer points:

- Father, thank You for the power of the Holy Spirit present in our lives to help us.
- Holy Spirit, help me to see how important this fruit is to my success as a witnessing Christian.
- Help me to be patient under trial and to develop the fruit of patience in my life, today and everyday.

In Jesus' Name.
Amen

Verses for the Day:

"Wherefore seeing we also are compassed about with so great a cloud of witnesses, let us lay aside every weight, and the sin which doth so easily beset us, and let us run with patience the race that is set before us, looking unto Jesus the author and finisher of our faith; who for the joy that was set before him endured the cross, despising the shame, and is set down at the right hand of the throne of God. For consider him that endured such contradiction of sinners against himself, lest ye be wearied and faint in your minds." (Heb 12:1-3)

Patience: Promoting Unity! (2)

- Patience is not passive; on the contrary it is active; it is concentrated strength
- Patience is the ability let go of your need for immediate gratification and be willing to wait.
- Patience is the trait that displays tolerance, compassion, understanding, and acceptance toward those who are slower than you in developing maturity, emotional freedom, and coping abilities.
- Patience is the ability to remain calm in the midst of turmoil because you know God is in control.

God's will for local bodies and the Body of Christ as a whole is that the individual members be in unity in the Spirit and in faith. Before He went to heaven his prayer for his disciples was, "My prayer for all of them is that they will be one, just as you and I are one, Father--that just as you are in me and I am in you, so they will be in us, and the world will believe you sent me." (John 17:21-23)

The Bible says, "He (Jesus) is the one who gave these gifts to the church: the apostles, the prophets, the evangelists, and the pastors and teachers. Their responsibility is to equip God's people to do his work and build up the church, the body of Christ, until we come to such unity in our faith and knowledge of God's Son that we will be mature and full grown in the Lord, measuring up to the full stature of Christ." (Eph 4:11-13)

> **A man's wisdom gives him patience; it is to his glory to overlook an offence.**
> **PROVERBS 19:11**

How would the fruit of patience or longsuffering help in promoting unity among believers? In the parable of the debt ridden servant (Matt 18:23-30) who appealed to his master to be patient with him, we see the master overlooked the debt of the servant even though in today's currency it would be in excess of five million pounds. In the same respect, it takes the fruit of longsuffering in the life of a believer to overlook and lovingly forgive the faults of one another. The reaction of the forgiven debt ridden servant to the debt owed him by his own fellow servant is more prevalent among believers in local churches today. His fellow servant fell down at his feet, and besought him, saying, have patience with me, and I will pay thee" (Matt 18:29) Because the forgiven servant lacked longsuffering, he was not able to overlook and forgive, which would have enabled him to release his fellow servant from the bondage of the debt, which in today's currency would be approximately ten pounds.

Contrary to what most Christians think, their individual faults are not the reason for strife and divisions among them, but their lack of the fruit of patience and longsuffering in their lives. Peace and harmony exists between Christians not because we are so perfect and incapable of error, but because Christ's nature (the fruit of longsuffering) will be reigning and ruling in our hearts and in our lives. Solomon's advice to his son was, "Let not mercy and kindness [shutting out all hatred and selfishness] and truth [shutting out all deliberate hypocrisy or falsehood] forsake you; bind them about your neck, write them upon the tablet of your heart." (Prov 3:3)

A.W. Tozer in "The Pursuit of God" wrote, "Has it ever occurred to you that one hundred pianos all turned to the same fork are automatically tuned to each other? They are of one accord by being tuned, not to each other, but to another standard to which each one must individually bow. So one hundred worshipers [meeting] together, each one looking away to Christ, are in heart nearer to each other than they could possibly be, were they to become 'unity' conscious and turn their eyes away from God to strive for closer fellowship".

Today, let walk as Paul urged you to walk. "Since God chose you to be the holy people whom He loves, you must clothe yourselves with tender-hearted mercy, kindness, humility, gentleness, and patience. You must make allowance for each other's faults and forgive the person who offends you. Remember, the Lord forgave you, so you must forgive others."

Prayer points:

- Father, thank You for showing me that unity is not a result of the absence of strife and division, but comes about when I allow the fruit of longsuffering to be demonstrated in my life.
- Help me to walk in patience and mercy towards others today.

In Jesus' Name.
Amen

Verses for the Day:

"I therefore, the prisoner of the Lord, beseech you that ye walk worthy of the vocation wherewith ye are called, with all lowliness and meekness, with longsuffering, forbearing one another in love; Endeavouring to keep the unity of the Spirit in the bond of peace." (Eph 4:1-3)

Patience: Possessing Your Possessions! (3)

- Patience is the ability to sit back and wait for an expected outcome without experiencing anxiety, tension, or frustration.
- Patience is the ability let go of your need for immediate gratification and be willing to wait.

A recent visit to Colorado opened my eyes to the overwhelming efforts made by the miners during the US gold rush. They fought through many challenges, hardships and the rocky terrain to possess the precious gold that many paid for dearly with their lives. It is through this same preserving, enduring spirit that believers need to possess their possessions and inheritance in Christ.

The writer of Hebrews encourages us with these words, "Instead, you will follow the example of those who are going to inherit God's promises because of their faith and patience. For example, there was God's promise to Abraham. Since there was no one greater to swear by, God took an oath in his own name, saying: "I will certainly bless you richly, and I will multiply your descendants into countless millions." Then Abraham waited patiently, and he received what God had promised. (Heb 6:12-15) Abraham obtained the promise of a son only after patiently enduring for a period of twenty five years. (Gen 12:4; 17:17) Have you ever believed for a promise of God? How long did you have to wait to see it manifested in your life? Have you ever given up on what you believed God for and settled for Plan B?

> **Have patience with all things, but first of all with yourself.**
> **ST FRANCIS DE SALES**

True faith, like true love, never gives up. Paul urges us in Eph 6 to "Be strong with the Lord's mighty power. Put on all of God's armour so that you will be able to stand firm against all strategies and tricks of the Devil. For we are not fighting against people made of flesh and blood, but against the evil rulers and authorities of the unseen world, against those mighty powers of darkness who rule this world, and against wicked spirits in the heavenly realms. Use every piece of God's armour to resist the enemy in the time of evil, so that after the battle you will still be standing firm. Stand your ground, putting on the sturdy belt of truth and the body armour of God's righteousness." The Word of God teaches us that after we have done all we know to do, then we must stand. After we have built up our faith and fasted and prayed and put on the whole armour of God, we must recognise the necessity and importance of standing. This is where many of us fail.

The writer of Hebrews admonishes, "Without wavering, let us hold tightly to the hope we say we have, for God can be trusted to keep his promise." (Heb 10:23) Jesus said, "Listen to me! You can pray for anything, and if you believe, you will have it." (Mark 11:24) Time is not a consideration in the prayer. Jesus said, "you will have it." Do you believe what He said? Then wait patiently. The fruit of longsuffering will enable us to stand and obtain the promises of God for our lives.

Today the promises of God are for all of us who believe. They are claimed by faith, and obtained by patience. I once read, "faith claims the promise, and patience receives the promise." May you stand firm and receive the promises of peace, prosperity, wholeness and healing in every area of your life.

Prayer points:

- Father, thank You for showing me why I need desperately to cultivate the fruit of longsuffering in my life.
- May I claim your promises by faith and patiently possess them one by one.
- Help me to display the fruit of patience in my life today.

In Jesus' Name.
Amen

Verse for the Day:

"That you do not become sluggish, but imitate those who through faith and patience inherit the promises." (Heb 6:12)

Day 17

Patience: How to Get It? (4)

- Endurance is "the capacity to remain firm under suffering without yielding to anger, resentment, despair or self pity.
- Patience is the ability to sit back and wait for an expected outcome without experiencing anxiety, tension, or frustration.
- By standing firm, you will win your souls.

If this fruit of longsuffering or patience is so key to is to producing endurance in our lives, walking in unity and receiving the promises of God, how do we cultivate and develop it in our lives?

The first way is by keeping the Word of God. The parable of the sower and the seed illustrates this point. The sower sowed the seed, and some fell by the wayside, some fell upon a rock and some fell amount thorns. None of this seed produced fruit, simply because it was not capable of growing to maturity. However, the seed that fell on good ground produced thirty, sixty and a hundredfold return. The 'good ground' constitutes Christians who hear the word of God and allow it to take root in their lives long enough to grow to maturity and produce fruit. God told Adam to 'keep the garden'. (Gen 2:15) Because Adam did not fulfil his God – given responsibility he lived on a lower level than God ever intended for his life.

The end of a matter is better than its beginning, and patience is better than pride.
ECCLESIASTES 7:8

The same is true for any of us who do not keep the Word the Lord entrusts to us – we will live on a lower spiritual plain than God ever intended for us to live on. Jesus admonished His followers to keep the Word and bring forth fruit with patience. (Luke 8:15) As we keep the Word and study the Word of God for ourselves, Hebrews 10:32 says, "the illumination of the Word of God produces endurance". It is after we are illuminated by the Word of God that we are capable of enduring even a vast opposition of afflictions.

Secondly, we cultivate the fruit of longsuffering or patience by experiencing trials and tribulation and responding to them in the right way with the right attitude. Paul wrote, And not only so, but we glory in tribulations also: knowing that tribulation works patience." (Rom 5:3) Knowing that patience or longsuffering is being developed in our lives through trials makes us able to glory even in the midst of them. "Dear brothers and sisters, whenever trouble comes your way, let it be an opportunity for joy. For when your faith is tested, your endurance has a chance to grow." (James 1:2-3) Those who wait on God during their trials develop patience; whereas those who worry though their trials only develop spiritual paralysis. Isaiah wrote of God, "He gives power to those who are tired and worn out; he offers strength to the weak. Even youths will become exhausted, and young men will give up. But those who wait on the LORD will find new strength. They will fly high on wings like eagles. They will run and not grow weary. They will walk and not faint." (Is 40:29-31) In times of trial those who are truly waiting on God are eagerly anticipating the manifestation of answer to their prayers.

We develop the fruit of patience by maintaining hope. Proverbs tells us that 'hope deferred makes the heart sick; but when the desire comes, it is a tree of life.! (Prov 13:12) Peter urges us to, "think clearly and exercise self-control. Look forward to the special blessings that will come to you at the return of Jesus Christ. (1 Peter 1:13) We need to keep hope alive in our hearts for ourselves, through our trials and for others. We must not give up on others or we will become bitter and short-tempered.

Using Abraham as our example, the Bible says "When God promised Abraham that he would become the father of many nations, Abraham believed him. God had also said, "Your descendants will be as numerous as the stars," even though such a promise seemed utterly impossible! And Abraham's faith did not weaken, even though he knew that he was too old to be a father at the age of one hundred and that Sarah, his wife, had never been able to have children."

May you cultivate the fruit of patience in your life as you keep the Word, be patient through trials and keeping the awesome hope we have alive in our hearts, today.

Prayer points:

- Father, thank You for showing me how important it is to develop the fruit of longsuffering in my life.
- May I be a 'good ground' Christian who keeps and studies the Word and bears good fruit.
- Help me to keep the right attitude and remain steady through trial knowing that all things work together for the good of those who trust in You.

In Jesus' Name.
Amen

Verse for the Day:

"For you have need of endurance, so that after you have done the will of God, you may receive the promise." (Hebrews 10:36)

Kindness precedes Goodness!

- Gentleness is what people see in a believer
- Goodness is what they outwardly experience from that believer.
- Without kindness there is no manifested goodness.
- For we are only as good (useful) to God as we are good (kind) to people.

Paul wrote, "But the fruit of the Spirit of God is ..... gentleness, goodness," (Gal 5:22)

According to W. E. Vine, one Greek Scholar has described 'gentleness', or 'kindness', as "a kindly disposition toward others," whereas 'goodness' is defined as "a kindly activity on their behalf." In other words, gentleness is what people see in a believer, and goodness is what they outwardly experience from that believer.

If a Christian therefore does not have a kindly disposition toward people, then he/she cannot possibly manifest goodness toward them. Without kindness there is no manifested goodness. This is especially true in the case of forgiveness: "Instead, be kind to each other, tender-hearted, forgiving one another, just as God through Christ has forgiven you. (Eph 4:32) Kindness brings a tender disposition, which is especially necessary in manifesting the good works of forgiveness.

> **No act of kindness, no matter how small, is wasted.**
> **AESOP**

Jesus spoke of these two fruits but called them different names. "You are the salt of the earth. But what good is salt if it has lost its flavour? Can you make it useful again? It will be thrown out and trampled underfoot as worthless. You are the light of the world-- like a city on a mountain, glowing in the night for all to see. Don't hide your light under a basket! Instead, put it on a stand and let it shine for all. In the same way, let your good deeds shine out for all to see, so that everyone will praise your heavenly Father. (Matt 5:13-16)

Salt is a type of the fruit of kindness, for it brings seasoning to the earth. How rare it is these days to find kind people. It is like finding an oasis in a desert. Typical of salt, a believer's kindness brings savour or seasoning to the earth. Light is a type of the fruit of goodness. He taught his followers, "Let your light so shine before men, that they may see your good works. When a believer's salt or kindness is savoury towards another, then his/her light will automatically shine through the manifestation of his/her good works.

Paul also recognised the precedence of kindness being the door out of which goodness can flow. (1 Thess 2:7-9) Jesus also taught that kindness must precede goodness. "But what good is salt if it has lost its flavour? Can you make it useful again? It will be thrown out and trampled underfoot as worthless". Without the spirit of kindness, what is the motive of your good works? We all know when someone goes good works towards us with ulterior motives! Without the seasoning, Jesus calls them worthless! The Greek word translated gentleness in Gal 5:22 is 'chrestotes', meaning 'usefulness'. A believer who loses his kindly disposition toward someone automatically loses his usefulness for God. Jesus said when this happens such a person might as well be cast out, and trodden under foot of men. (Matt 5:13)

The degree to which we are useful to God is determined by the degree to which the fruit of kindness has been developed in our lives, for we are only as good (useful) to God as we are good (kind) to people.

The fruit of kindness must be developed in your life if you are to shine as a light in the world today.

Prayer points:

- Father, thank You for Your Word that brings me knowledge.
- May I apply that knowledge in my life which makes it 'wisdom from God'.

- Help me to understand how important the fruits of kindness and goodness are in my life to enable me to be the salt and light of the world.

In Jesus' Name.
Amen

<u>Verse for the Day</u>:

"In everything you do, stay away from complaining and arguing, so that no one can speak a word of blame against you. You are to live clean, innocent lives as children of God in a dark world full of crooked and perverse people. Let your lives shine brightly before them." (Phil 2:14-15)

Kindness: You Are The Salt of the Earth! (2)

- Salt is a purifier and a preservative of that which can rot or decay.
- Salt is universal and 'no respecter or persons'.
- Salt has antiseptic and healing qualities.

The fruit of kindness is what enables you to be the salt of the earth. Being salt of the earth performs three spiritual functions which may be compared to three of the many physical attributes of salt.

Firstly, like salt, the fruit of kindness is comparable to the purifying quality of salt on the earth. Salt can be used as a fertiliser to prepare soil for bearing fruit. In the same way, kindness prepares the hearts of unbelievers for receiving the implantation of the seed of reconciliation. Paul wrote to Titus, "Once we, too, were foolish and disobedient. We were misled by others and became slaves to many wicked desires and evil pleasures. Our lives were full of evil and envy. We hated others, and they hated us. But then God our Saviour showed us his kindness and love. He saved us, not because of the good things we did, but because of his mercy. He washed away our sins and gave us a new life through the Holy Spirit." (Titus 3:3-5)

Those who experience the new birth do so because they first experience the loving kindness of God, for kindness is a forerunner of regeneration. As the salt of the earth, you are God's expression of His kindness and goodness to the world. Peter wrote that unbelievers would be won to the Lord simply by watching the 'behaviour' of believers and beholding their 'chaste' manner of life. (1 Peter 3:1-4)

If you want to lift yourself up, lift up someone else.
BOOKER T WASHINGTON

Secondly, like salt, there is a universal quality of the fruit of kindness. No matter what type of restaurant you eat at, salt is universally identical. Just as salt is 'no respecter or persons, so also is the fruit of kindness, regardless of how unsavoury a person or a situation might be, it always has the same quality and always produces the same flavour. James 2:9 reminds us, "But if you pay special attention to the rich, you are committing a sin, for you are guilty of breaking that law." Jesus reminds us "Salt is good for seasoning. But if it loses its flavour, how do you make it salty again? You must have the qualities of salt among yourselves and live in peace with each other." (Mark 9:50) We need to remain salty not only towards Christians, but towards unbelievers and towards our own spouses and family.

The fruit of kindness is comparable to the antiseptic quality of salt, which makes it useful as a mouthwash. Once developed in your life it will enable you to fulfil Ephesians 4:29. "Don't use foul or abusive language. Let everything you say be good and helpful, so that your words will be an encouragement to those who hear them." "Let your speech always be with grace, seasoned with salt, that you may know how you ought to answer each one." (Col 4:6)

The three effects of the fruit of kindness on your mouth will be:

1. It will enable you to turn away from wrath. "A soft answer turns away wrath, but a harsh word stirs up anger." (Prov 15:1)

2. It will enable you to withhold wounds. "The words of a talebearer are like tasty trifles, and they go down into the inmost body." (Prov 18:8)

3. It will enable you to cease strife or contention. "Where there is no wood, the fire goes out; and where there is no talebearer, strife ceases. (Prov 26:20)

How salty are you today?

Prayer Points

- Father, thank You for Your Word that brings me knowledge.
- May my words be salted with the fruit of kindness.
- May I speak pleasant words that bring health rather than harm to others.

- May I promote healing with my tongue.

In Jesus' Name.
Amen

Verse for the Day:

"Pleasant words are like a honeycomb, Sweetness to the soul and health to the bones." (Prov 16:24)

Kindness: Who Offended You? (3)

- Light always dispels darkness.
- Beware the bushel of offence that comes to hide the light?
- How to deal with offences.

Jesus wrote of you, "You are the light of the world. A city that is set on a hill cannot be hidden. Nor do they light a lamp and put it under a basket, but on a lampstand, and it gives light to all who are in the house. Let your light so shine before men, that they may see your good works and glorify your Father in heaven." (Matt 5:14-16)

The light that is lit within you when you are born again is your spirit. According to Proverbs 20:27, "The spirit of man is the candle of the Lord." It is through your spirit that the light of God floods in. Jesus wants the candles that He has lit to be placed on candlesticks so that light will shine to all that are in the house. Why? "That they will see your good works and glorify our Father in Heaven."

Jesus warns however that we should guard against bushels or baskets that would prevent our lights from shining. Bushels and baskets are anything that would come against you and distort your disposition in order to affect your kindness, which inevitably quenches your goodness. Many of us start the

> To err is human, to forgive divine.
> **ALEXANDER POPE**

Christian walk with kindness but after a period of time that flame within us grows dimmer and dimmer. Like the church of Ephesus in Rev 2:4, 5, we lose the passion of our first love.

The first basket or bushel that comes to distort or affect our light is 'offence'. As soon as a believer gets offended, his disposition changes instantly: Solomon wrote, "It's harder to make amends with an offended friend than to capture a fortified city. Arguments separate friends like a gate locked with iron bars." (Prov 18:19) An offended believer displays contention, not kindness. Regardless of who has offended him/her – whether it was the pastor or minister, a fellow believer, or someone outside the church. According to Jesus, two consequences of becoming offended are hatred and betrayal. (Matt 24:9, 10) 'To betray', means 'turning against what was once followed.' Generally most people know when someone is faking kindness and when it is truly flowing from the depths of their heart. We must avoid offences – taking offence, as well as giving it! How do we do this?

Firstly, Jesus tells us that 'offences will definitely come'. He urges us not to take offence or be offended by soaking yourself in the Word of God. By doing this you will find yourself less likely to get your feeling hurt. David wrote, "Great peace have they which love thy law: and nothing shall offend them." (Ps 119:165)

Secondly, we overcome offence by walking in the love of God. According to 1 Corinthians 13:4-7, Love is not easily offended. Praying in the Spirit keeps you in the love of God – that love which bears and endures all things. When you get offended, it is a clear indication that your love is not yet perfected.

Thirdly to overcome being offended is by ministering love to those who may end up offending us. Jesus told his disciples, "I say to you, love your enemies, bless those who curse you, do good to those who hate you, and pray for those who spitefully use you and persecute you." Jesus did this to Judas when he washed his feet and left us an example of how to treat others. (John 13:15)

The temptation to be offended will always be there because we are human, however as we learn to minister to those who abuse us, we will walk spiritually free from the restraining satanic tool of hurt feelings. Replacing hurt feelings with the love of God frustrates the plan of the enemy and implements the plan of God. Paul urges believers to "Be not overcome of evil, but overcome evil with good." (Rom 12:19-21) May you walk in the love of God today to those who have offended you?

Prayer Points

- Father, thank You that You thought about all the situations that could happen to me.

- Help me to walk in forgiveness and love towards those who have offended me.
- May I pray for those who have hurt my feelings and bless them when I can.
- May I overcome evil with good today.

In Jesus' Name.
Amen

Verse for the Day:

"Great peace have they who love Your law; nothing shall offend them or make them stumble." (Ps 119:165)

Kindness: As Bold As A Lion! (4)

- The righteous are as bold as a lion.
- You become like who you hang around with.
- Developing boldness.

"Let your light so shine before men, that they may see your good works and glorify your Father in heaven." (Matt 5:16) Jesus warns however that we should guard against bushels or baskets that would prevent our lights from shining.

Apart from the bushel or basket of offence that comes to distort or affect your light, another major bushel in the Body of Christ is intimidation. "For God has not given us the spirit of fear; but of power, and of love, and of a sound mind." (2 Tim 1:7) The word 'fear' actually means 'timidity. God has not given you a timid or shy spirit.

Timidity is a thief that would rob you of your potential for goodness. It will have a negative effect on the power, love and sound mind which have been promised by God. You may have a beautiful spirit of kindness but because of timidity that spirit is hindered from being manifested in your life and does not come forth. The Bible tells us that "the wicked man flees though no one pursues, but the righteous are as bold as a lion." (Prov 28:1) As a Christian, made righteousness through Christ and not of our own works, God intended that His children be blessed both with righteousness and boldness. Sometimes you need to battle with timidity in order to claim your rightful inheritance of boldness.

> **The measure of love is compassion, the measure of compassion is kindness.**
> **ANONYMOUS**

How do we develop this holy boldness that is our inheritance?

Firstly we must spend time with the Lord. People tend to be like those with whom they associate most closely and most frequently. "The members of the council were amazed when they saw the boldness of Peter and John, for they could see that they were ordinary men who had had no special training. They also recognized them as men who had been with Jesus." (Acts 4:13) As is said, "show me your friends and I will tell you who you are!" The reason Peter and John possessed such boldness is that they had been with the Lion: "The lion has roared--tremble in fear! The Sovereign LORD has spoken--I dare not refuse to proclaim his message! (Amos 3:8) When you know that you have heard the voice of the Lord you will be bold to speak it forth clearly and confidently and not be hesitant.

Secondly, to develop boldness you can simply ask God for it. James told us, "You have not because you ask not." (James 4:2) This is exactly what the disciples did in Acts 4:29, 30. God answered their prayer and gave them so much boldness that the room they were in was shaken!

The third way we can become bold is by praying for one another. Paul asked the church in Ephesus to pray for all saints and especially for boldness for him. "And pray for me, too. Ask God to give me the right words as I boldly explain God's secret plan that the Good News is for the Gentiles, too. I am in chains now for preaching this message as God's ambassador. But pray that I will keep on speaking boldly for him, as I should. (Eph 6:19-20)

Jesus' life and death was the manifestation of God's kindness and goodness to the world. Jesus was always kind to the people, and He ever did acts of goodness on their behalf. Today, may you be like Jesus.

Prayer Points

- Father, thank You for showing me that it is your will for me to be as bold as a lion.
- May I spend time with you so I may be confident in what I say and do.
- Help me to pray for boldness to confront and face the situations and circumstances that come my way.
- May I pray for all saints that they exhibit the spirit of boldness today.

In Jesus' Name.
Amen

Verse for the Day:

"For God has not given us the spirit of fear; but of power, and of love, and of a sound mind." (2 Tim 1:7)

Faithfulness: An Excellent Spirit!

- Faithful followers – A dying breed?
- You are faithful in relation to trust placed in you by others and by God.

The concept of 'faithfulness' is becoming more and more obsolete in today's world although it is listed as one of the nine fruit of the Spirit of God living within you. "But the fruit of the Spirit is faith…" (Gal 5:22) It is becoming more and more obvious that to walk in faithfulness is almost impossible without the power of God operating in your life.

The best translation of the Greek word rendered faith in the KJV is actually the word faithfulness. English is a strange language. You would think that the words "full of faith" and "faithful" would be the same thing. They are not. They are related, but they are not the same thing. To be full of faith is to have an abundance of faith. To be faithful is to keep the faith. It is being true to the trust placed in us by others and by God. You are faithful in relation to trust placed in you by others and by God.

> **Faithfulness is consecration in overalls.**
> **EVELYN UNDERHILL**
> **(1875-1941)**

The Webster dictionary defines faithful as being steadfast in affection or allegiance; firm in adherence to promises or in observance of duty; true to the facts, to a standard, or to an original. Other synonyms are loyal, conscientious, constant, staunch, steadfast and resolute . Faithful implies unswerving adherence to a person or thing or to the oath or promise by which a tie was contracted.

We read about Daniel, an Old Testament example of faithfulness. "Darius the Mede decided to divide the kingdom into 120 provinces, and he appointed a prince to rule over each province. The king also chose Daniel and two others as administrators to supervise the princes and to watch out for the king's interests. Daniel soon proved himself more capable than all the other administrators and princes. Because of his great ability, the king made plans to place him over the entire empire. Then the other administrators and princes began searching for some fault in the way Daniel was handling his affairs, but they couldn't find anything to criticize. He was faithful and honest and always responsible." (Dan 6:1-4)

Daniel had such an excellent spirit about him that he just stood out from all the others around him. Verse 4 tells us that it was faithfulness that made him stand out. His enemies looked for fault in Daniel but found none, because he was faithful in everything that he did. His faithfulness showed in the following areas:

1. He was faithful to his occupation. He was the third ruler in the kingdom of Babylon.
2. He was faithful in his position in serving the king. He was president over the Median-Persian empire, next to the king.
3. He was faithful to prayer. Daniel prayed three times every day.
4. He was faithful to God.
   a. In chapter 1, he was faithful in that he did not defile himself with the king's meat or drink.
   b. He was faithful in the den of lions. Because Daniel was faithful to God, God was faithful to him and delivered him. Some of you may feel like you've been put into the den of lions...don't give up...don't quit...don't stop praying...don't stop fasting...be faithful to God and He will be faithful to you.

The Lord spoke through David in Ps 101:6 saying "My eyes shall [look with favour] upon the faithful of the land, that they may dwell with me; he who walks blamelessly, he shall minister to me." When the Lord finds a faithful believer, He focuses His undivided attention upon him. God is looking for this character quality in his people. As you allow the power of the Holy Spirit to work in you, may the fruit of faithfulness to God be manifest in your life today.

Prayer Points

- Father, thank You for showing me that it is your will for me to be faithful to you, my employer, my church, my spouse and my family.

- May I be faithful to live according to your word and will for my life today.
- May I develop an excellent spirit, like Daniel had, through faithfulness to those who have placed trust in me.
- May the fruit of faithfulness be displayed in my life today.

In Jesus' Name.
Amen

Verses for the Day:

"And so, dear brothers and sisters who belong to God and are bound for heaven, think about this Jesus whom we declare to be God's Messenger and High Priest. For he was faithful to God, who appointed him, just as Moses served faithfully and was entrusted with God's entire house." (Heb 3:1-2)

Faithfulness: Use It Or Lose It! (2)

- One of the functions of the fruit of faithfulness in our lives is to equip you to exercise stewardship over God's goods.
- God has entrusted each one of us with His 'gifts of grace'.
- Examples of the dangers of unfaithfulness

"But the fruit of the spirit is …..faith." Gal 5:22. The best translation of the Greek word rendered faith in the King James Version is actually the word faithfulness. I believe every Christian is hoping one day to hear the Lord say to us personally and individually, "Well done, you good and faithful servant." (Matt 25:21)

True faith shows up in faithfulness. Not everyone can sing or preach, but all can be faithful.

A certain king needed a faithful servant and had to choose between two candidates for the office. He took both at fixed wages and told them to fill a basket with water from a nearby well, saying that he would come in the evening to inspect their work. After dumping one or two buckets of water into the basket, one of the men said, "What is the good of doing this useless work? As soon as we pour the water in, it runs out the sides." The other answered, "But we have our wages, haven't we? The use is the master's business, not ours. He is a wise King, and must have his own purpose that we do not understand." "I'm not going to do such fool's work," replied the complainer. Throwing down his bucket, he went away. The other man continued until he had drained the well. Looking down into it, he saw something shining at the bottom - it was a diamond ring. "Now I see the use of pouring water into the basket!" he exclaimed. "If the bucket had brought up the ring before the well was dry, it would have been filtered out in the basket. The King was looking for his diamond. Our work was not useless." The King found his most faithful servant!

If faithfulness is a fruit of the Holy Spirit living on the inside of you, it means faithfulness is a characteristic that is important to God.

The first reason why we need to develop faithfulness in our lives as part of our character is to equip you to exercise stewardship over God's goods. God created Adam for fellowship, but also to care for the Garden of Eden. (Gen 2:4-8, 15; 3:23-24) Man was made to be a recipient of, and a ruler of God's creation. We all know what happened to Adam. His unfaithfulness to God caused God to drive him out from that which he was to rule over. God does not want you to lose the privilege of ruling over the things He has for you in the Spirit.

The parable of the talents in Matthew 25:14-30 shows that God expects us to be diligent and faithful with everything that He gives us and expects us to use and increase whatever we have. It is a spiritual principle that God will take His goods from the unfaithful and give them to the faithful. According to verse 29, everyone who has been faithful will receive more, but he who has been unfaithful will lose even what he does have. Verse 28 indicates that the goods of those unfaithful will be taken from them by the Lord and given to someone who will use them wisely for the sake of the Lord's kingdom.

Esau sold his birthright to Jacob because it was not his heart's desire to be faithful to God. (Heb 12:12-17) Saul forfeited his kingship because he proved himself unfaithful to that calling, and the Lord removed his anointing from him and placed it upon David, the young shepherd boy He knew would be faithful. (1 Sam 16:14) Because the nation of Israel was not faithful with the revelation of the promised Messiah, the Lord took the revelation from them and gave it to the Gentiles, a people who would accept it and be faithful with it. (Matt 21:23)
Today, God is still looking for faithful people to whom He can entrust His goods. According to Proverbs 28:20, "A faithful man shall abound with blessings, but he who makes haste to be rich [at any cost] shall not go unpunished."

Prayer Points:

- Father, help me to be faithful with the gift/gifts that You have blessed me with.

- I repent of any talent, ability or gifting that has remained dormant in my life or I have neglected to use in my life.
- Help me to understand that my gifts are not my own but are to be used to be a blessing to others and the body of Christ.
- Help me develop faithfulness with all You have entrusted me with today.

In Jesus' Name.
Amen

Verses for the Day:

"Who is a faithful, sensible servant, to whom the master can give the responsibility of managing his household and feeding his family? If the master returns and finds that the servant has done a good job, there will be a reward. I assure you, the master will put that servant in charge of all he owns." (Matt 24:45 - 47)

Faithfulness: Are You A Moses, A Joshua or an Aaron? (3)

- Can you be trusted to carry out instructions?
- Are you a faithful, sensible servant, to whom the master can give the responsibility of managing his household and feeding his family?

Does the fruit of faithfulness manifest in your life?

In Exodus 24 we look at the faithfulness of three people, Moses, Joshua. Aaron and Hur. The Lord said to Moses, ""Come up here to me, and bring along Aaron, Nadab, Abihu, and seventy of Israel's leaders. All of them must worship at a distance. You alone, Moses, are allowed to come near to the LORD. The others must not come too close. And remember, none of the other people are allowed to climb on the mountain at all. When Moses had announced to the people all the teachings and regulations the LORD had given him, they answered in unison, "We will do everything the LORD has told us to do." Moses carried out the instructions he had been given by God. Later on in that same chapter God give Moses another set of instructions: "And the LORD said to Moses, "Come up to me on the mountain. Stay there while I give you **Faithfulness is the unconditional commitment to love and serve.** the tablets of stone that I have inscribed with my instructions and commands. Then you will teach the people from them." So Moses and his assistant Joshua climbed up the mountain of God. Moses told the other leaders, "Stay here and wait for us until we come back. If there are any problems while I am gone, consult with Aaron and Hur, who are here with you." Moses was a man faithful to carry out instructions given to him by the Lord. (Ex 24)

While Moses was up on the mountain with God and Joshua had been instructed by Moses to wait half way up the mountain, we read, "When Moses failed to come back down the mountain right away, the people went to Aaron." "Look," they said, "make us some gods who can lead us. This man Moses, who brought us here from Egypt, has disappeared. We don't know what has happened to him. So Aaron said, "Tell your wives and sons and daughters to take off their gold earrings, and then bring them to me." (Ex 32) What happened next is history. Aaron followed the instructions of the people and made a golden calf for them. While Moses was still with the Lord, God told him exactly what the people were up to that he had left in the care of Aaron and Hur. Joshua on the other hand had not moved out of his delegated position. Moses had to intercede on behalf of Aaron for God's wrath to be averted.

Are you faithful in a position of responsibility you have been given by God as a father or mother, a husband or a wife, by an employer or line manager, by a pastor/minister or team leader at church? How do you handle your God-given instructions through His Word? How do you behave when someone has delegated a duty or task to you? Are you faithful to carry out the instructions of whoever was in authority over you in that respect? Do you disregard instructions because you have a better idea? Do you heed the instructions of those you have been placed over or do you faithfully carry out the instructions of those in authority even when you do not understand or agree with every instruction?

Are you a Moses, a Joshua or an Aaron? True to His character, God passed on Moses' role to Joshua because of his faithfulness. Don't expect God to increase your role or job or your ministry until you prove faithful at where you're at. Don't expect God to you use you as lighthouse tomorrow when He can't even use you as a candle today. Be faithful in what you've got. You may only have one talent, but be faithful in that one. God does not ask how many talents we have; he asks for faithfulness.

When it comes to your local church or assembly, it does not matter whether you pastor the largest church in town, or if you're the door opener in the smallest church, just as long as you are faithful in what you have been asked to do. The faithfulness is all that matters.

John Oxenham wrote:
"Is your place a small place?
Tend it with care!-He set you there?

Is your place a large place?
Guard it with care!-He set you there.
Whate'er your place, it is
Not yours alone, but his
Who set you there."

Today, God is still looking for faithful people to whom He can entrust His goods. May you be that faithful one today.

Prayer Points:

- Father, help me to be faithful where you have placed me.
- I repent of any area where I have failed to prove faithful, whether in my family role, my job or in my local church responsibility.
- Help me to understand that promotion does not come from the East or the West but comes from You alone.
- Help me to manifest the fruit of faithfulness in my life today.

In Jesus' Name.
Amen

Verses for the Day:

"Lift not up your horn on high: speak not with a stiff neck. For promotion cometh neither from the east, nor from the west, nor from the south. But God is the judge: he putteth down one, and setteth up another." (Ps 75:5-7)

Faithfulness: A Closer Walk! (4)

* Do you want to hear God clearly?
* Are you prepared to do God's will for your life?
* Is His kingdom come and His will be done in your life the highest priority?

Another reason to cultivate faithfulness in our life as a believer enables you to experience close fellowship – not talking about relationship – with the father. Take Moses for example:

"While they were at Hazeroth, Miriam and Aaron criticized Moses because he had married a Cushite woman. They said, "Has the LORD spoken only through Moses? Hasn't he spoken through us, too?" But the LORD heard them. Then the LORD descended in the pillar of cloud and stood at the entrance of the Tabernacle. "Aaron and Miriam!" he called, and they stepped forward. And the LORD said to them, "Now listen to me! Even with prophets, I the LORD communicate by visions and dreams. But that is not how I communicate with my servant Moses. He is entrusted with my entire house. I speak to him face to face, directly and not in riddles! He sees the LORD as he is. Should you not be afraid to criticize him?" (Num 12:1,2,5-8)

> **He who is faithful over a few things is a lord of cities.**
> **LUKE 19:17**

Verse 8 describes the result of Moses' faithfulness – God spoke to him mouth to mouth, even apparently. Apparently means God spoke to him in a clear voice that was completely understandable to his mind. God wants to speak clearly to His people but you need to be faithful to pay attention to what He says.

Jesus said in John 5:30, "I can of mine own self do nothing: as I hear, I judge: and my judgment is just; because I seek not mine own will, but the will of the Father which hath sent me. Jesus had an intimate relationship with the Father that every time He was faced with a situation He clearly heard the voice of God and immediately discerned what to do. A few examples we read about are:

1. When the woman caught in adultery was brought to Him, He stooped down and knew exactly how to respond to the situation. The scribes and Pharisees became convicted of their own sinfulness and gradually left, one by one.
2. Jesus could hear the Fathers voice so clearly because of His faithfulness. Hebrews 3:2 compares the faithfulness of Jesus with the faithfulness of Moses. "For he was faithful to God, who appointed him, just as Moses served faithfully and was entrusted with God's entire house." He was faithful to the one who appointed him, just as Moses was faithful in all God's house. We believers today will perceive the clarity of God's voice only as we are faithful to obey His commands and thus fulfil His will.
3. Jesus said, "My sheep hear my voice, and I know them, and they follow me." God does not speak to believers just so they can say they have heard His voice; He speaks to those He knows He can trust to follow Him.

May you develop the fruit of faithfulness to His will in your life so you can hear God clearly today.

Prayer Points:

- Father, thank You for insight and wisdom through Your word.
- May I place being faithful to your will for my life over my desire to be comfortable.
- You are interested in developing the Christ like nature in me by Your Spirit.
- Your will be done in my life and not mine.

In Jesus' Name.
Amen

Verse for the Day:

"Moses was certainly faithful in God's house, but only as a servant. His work was an illustration of the truths God would reveal later. But Christ, the faithful Son, was in charge of the entire household." (Heb 3:5)

Faithfulness: Pleasing To God! (5)

- God is more interested in faithfulness than He is in accomplishment.
- Jesus said that He always did those things which pleased His Father.
- Vance Havner says, "God is faithful, and He expects His people to be faithful.

According to the New Testament, faith pleases God: So, you see, it is impossible to please God without faith. Anyone who wants to come to him must believe that there is a God and that he rewards those who sincerely seek him. (Heb 11:6). The word faith is the Greek word 'Pistis' meaning firmness, fidelity, faithfulness - the character of one who can be relied on. According to Apostle Paul, and four times through the Bible, we are reminded that "The just shall live by faith." (Rom 1:17) In other words, the just or righteous ones are to live by pleasing God. We should be faithful because Jesus is Faithful.

> **A faithful man will be richly blessed, but one eager to get rich will not go unpunished.**
> **PROVERBS 28:20**

Many believers read chapter 11 of Hebrews which chronicles the exploits of the saints of God and marvel at the great faith of these men and women of old. In reality, what is being emphasized in that passage is not their great faith, but how they pleased God because of their great faithfulness?

Many believers today have made a golden calf out of faith. Their attitude seems to be: "let's develop our faith so we can get all these great things! Those who have this view point have lost sight of the root meaning of the word faith, which is faithfulness. Many get weary on their Christian walk because they are not standing to please God but standing to get a desired result. (Pro 23:13)

From the parable of the talents we read and hear the response of the Father to those who had used their talents. "The master was full of praise. `Well done, my good and faithful servant. You have been faithful in handling this small amount, so now I will give you many more responsibilities. Let's celebrate together!' (Matt 25:21) Clearly the third function of the fruit of faithfulness in our lives is to enable us to experience the joy of pleasing the Father. We can see that faithfulness on the part of a believer produces joy and appreciation within the heart of his master. In John 8:9 Jesus said that He always did those things which pleased His Father. Jesus was always faithful. Being faithful to God should be the most important goal in the life of a Christian, yet so many times we become so busy doing things for God that we are merely doing our own works in His name.

God is more interested in faithfulness than He is in accomplishment. His concern is not how much his children achieve in life as much as it is whether or not they are doing what He has told them to do. Proverbs 25:13 "As the cold of snow in the time of harvest, so is a faithful messenger to them that send him: for he refreshes the soul of his masters. God is totally refreshed when He finds a faithful messenger.

Vance Havner says, "God is faithful, and He expects His people to be faithful. God's Word speaks of faithful servants, faithful in a few things, faithful in the least, faithful in the Lord, faithful ministers. And all points up that day when He will say, "Well done, thou good and faithful servant." "What terrible times we have in our churches trying to keep people faithful in attendance and loyalty! How we reward and picnic and coax and tantalize church members into doing things they don't want to do but which they would do if they loved God! The only service that counts is faithful service. "True faith shows up in faithfulness. Not everyone can sing or preach, but all can be faithful."

The church of Jesus Christ must come to understand that the word faith means faithfulness and that the only reason to stand in faith is that by so doing we are being faithful to God, and therefore pleasing Him.

Prayer Points:

- Father, thank You for showing me that being faithful in the little things, in the least things and responsibilities You have entrusted to me through others pleases You.
- May I place being faithful to your will for my life over my desire to be comfortable.
- You are interested in developing the Christ like nature in me by Your Spirit.
- May I live to honour You today.

In Jesus' Name.
Amen

Verses for the Day:

"And even when you do ask, you don't get it because your whole motive is wrong--you want only what will give you pleasure. What do you think the Scriptures mean when they say that the Holy Spirit, whom God has placed within us, jealously longs for us to be faithful." (James 4: 3, 5)

Day 27

Faithfulness: With the Little! (6)

- How do we cultivate and develop the fruit of faithfulness.
- Possessions increase as a person's proven responsibility increases.
- Areas in which God expects our faithfulness.

The first way in which we may cultivate and develop the fruit of faithfulness is by being faithful in that which is least.   Jesus said, "He that is faithful in that which is least is faithful also in much: and he that is unjust in the least is unjust also in much." (Luke 16:10) Least is what you already have in your possession. Are you faithful with the little that you have? It is a strong spiritual principle that when you demonstrate that you are faithful with the least of your possessions, God can then bestow more important possessions upon you. Possessions increase as a person's proven responsibility increases.   Here are areas in which the Bible requires us to be faithful:

> **Now it is required that those who have been given a trust must prove faithful.**
> **1 COR 4:2**

A.   Have you been faithful in your fulfilment of past vows to God? (Eccl 5:4-6)

B.   Faithful in our family life. God trusted Abraham because he was faithful in the area of his family. (Gen 18:16-19) Start with your own family. "For if a man know not how to rule his own house, how shall he take care of the church of God?" (1 Tim 3:5)

- Husbands: Do you love your wife as Christ loved the church Eph 5:25
- Wives: Are you subject to your own husband as to the Lord? Eph 5:24
- Parents who are looking for a ministry together should ask themselves, "Are we training up our children in the way they should go?" (Prov 22:6)

- Children should ask themselves, "Am I obeying my parents in the Lord?" (Eph 6:1)

C.   Have you been faithful in using your talents and gifts in church. You may only have one talent, but be faithful in that one. Don't be jealous because another has 5 or 3 talents and you only have one. God does not ask how many talents we have; he asks for faithfulness with what you have. Paul was faithful before he was put into the ministry. "And I thank Christ Jesus our Lord, who hath enabled me, for that he counted me faithful, putting me into the ministry." (1 Tim. 1:12)

Paul told Timothy, "Timothy, don't waste your time trying to make teachers out of those who aren't even being faithful now. If they don't want to be faithful in just being a Christian, they don't need to be in ministry." He wrote, "And the things that thou hast heard of me among many witnesses, the same commit thou to faithful men/women, who shall be able to teach others also" (2 Tim 2:2)

D.   Are you faithful in your work?
"And if you have not proved faithful in that which belongs to another [whether God or man], who will give you that which is your own [that is, the true riches]? (Luke 16:12)
"You slaves must obey your earthly masters in everything you do. Try to please them all the time, not just when they are watching you. Obey them willingly because of your reverent fear of the Lord. Work hard and cheerfully at whatever you do, as though you were working for the Lord rather than for people." (Col 3:22-23) How can we be faithful with our work?

1. Most employers would rather have somebody without any education but was faithful and dedicated working for them than an unfaithful college graduate.
2. Get a job and stick with it.
3. Proverbs 28:20 says, "A faithful man shall abound with blessings"
4. Be on time.

5. Go to work.
6. Don't rob your boss man of five minutes that he paid your for.

Prayer Points:

* Father, thank You for showing me that being faithful in the little things, in the least things and responsibilities You have entrusted to me through others is important to You.
* May I continue and remain faithful in that which You have blessed and entrusted me with at present.

In Jesus' Name.
Amen

Verses for the Day:

"Unless you are faithful in small matters, you won't be faithful in large ones. If you cheat even a little, you won't be honest with greater responsibilities. And if you are untrustworthy about worldly wealth, who will trust you with the true riches of heaven?" (Luke 16:10-11)

Faithful In Finances! (7)

- You cannot serve both God and money.
- Money is the least of things that God expects us to be faithful with.
- Three ways money separates people's affections from God.

Another way in which we can develop the fruit of faithfulness is by being faithful with money which the bible refers to as 'unrighteous mammon' (Luke 16:11) and 'filthy lucre' (1 Tim 3:3)

Jesus told a story to his disciples about the rich man who hired a manager to take care of his financial affairs. We know that the manager was dishonest and was about to be fired. The manager made agreements with all the people who owed his master money. Many wonder at how Jesus or the rich master could commend or admire the dishonest rascal for being so shrewd and using the financial situation to safeguard his own future. God has entrusted us with financial resources in this life. The Bible makes it clear that 'it is God who gives us the power to prosper and to produce wealth. He gives us life itself!

> **And if you are untrustworthy about worldly wealth, who will trust you with the true riches of heaven?**
> **LUKE 16:11**

Just as the dishonest servant used the money to win favour for the future, so also Jesus tells us to, "Use your worldly resources to benefit others and make friends. In this way, your generosity stores up a reward for you in heaven." (Luke 16:9) He was not saying believers must be crooked, as many would like to believe, He was saying that we should use our finances for eternal purposes. Sow into our future in eternity. Store up our treasures in heaven.

To God, money is the least thing that He expects us to be faithful with. What are the true riches that God wants to entrust us with? They are the lives of precious souls for whom He shed the blood of His own dear Son. Jesus said, "And if you are untrustworthy about worldly wealth, who will trust you with the true riches of heaven?

And if you are not faithful with other people's money, why should you be trusted with money of your own? "No one can serve two masters. For you will hate one and love the other, or be devoted to one and despise the other. You cannot serve both God and money." (Luke 16;11-13) There is an uncanny correlation between a person's faithfulness to God and his attitude toward money. You can tell where a person's heart is by how they use their money. There is no other substance on the face of the earth which alienates people's affections away from God more than money does.

Here are three ways money separates people's affections from God:

The first way is in our thoughts. Many have the attitude that it all belongs to them since they worked for it! The Bible reminds us that 'the earth is the Lord's and everything that is within it belongs to Him.' Many believers find that money, how to get it, how to use it, how to stretch it, how to pay bills, takes up most of their thought life. Jesus knew that money would play an important part in the end times as the gospel requires loving Christians to fund it's being spread. Jesus said, "He will give you all you need from day to day if you live for him and make the Kingdom of God your primary concern. "So don't worry about tomorrow, for tomorrow will bring its own worries. Today's trouble is enough for today." (Matt 6:33-34)

The second way in which money separates people's affections from God is in our time. Jesus reminds us believers, "But you shouldn't be so concerned about perishable things like food. Spend your energy seeking the eternal life that I, the Son of Man, can give you. For God the Father has sent me for that very purpose." (John 6:27)

The third way in which money separates people's affections from God is in our accumulation and possession of it. "Every man should give according as he purposes in his heart, so let him give; not grudgingly or of necessity: for God loves a cheerful giver." (2 Cor 9:7) God wants us to give to His kingdom cheerfully and with enthusiasm. God will gladly bestow the 'true riches' upon anyone who gives with the attitude, "I'm always happy to give my money to the Lord; after all it all belongs to him anyhow!".

May the Spirit of the Lord help you today to be faithful to Him with your finances!

Prayer Points:

- Father, thank You for reminding me about the power You have given me to prosper and make wealth.
- May I honour You with my finances and sow towards eternal purposes in accordance with Your will.

In Jesus' Name.
Amen

Verses for the Day:

"Honour the LORD with your wealth and with the best part of everything your land produces. Then He will fill your barns with grain, and your vats will overflow with the finest wine." (Prov 3:9-10)

Faithful: Christ In You! (8)

• God's indwelling presence helps you develop the fruit of faithfulness.

• 12 promises for you about God's faithfulness.

"Then I saw heaven opened, and a white horse was standing there. And the one sitting on the horse was named Faithful and True." (Rev 19:11) Jesus was faithful in working His Father's work on the cross. Jesus said, "And the one who sent me is with me--he has not deserted me. For I always do those things that are pleasing to him." (John 8:29) Jesus had a conscious awareness of the Father's presence with him and he always did things that delighted the Father; He pleased God with His faithfulness. As Christians, we should be faithful to the will and word of God because it is a trait of Christ. If we are not faithful to God, we are not Christ like. Oswald Chambers wrote, "Watch where Jesus went. The one dominant note in his life was to do his Father's will. His is not the way of wisdom or of success, but the way of faithfulness."

Faithfulness is love's habit.

Being aware of God's indwelling presence helps you develop the fruit of faithfulness. Paul wrote, "For this is the secret: Christ lives in you, and this is your assurance that you will share in his glory." (Col 1:27) John wrote, "All who proclaim that Jesus is the Son of God have God living in them, and they live in God. (1 John 4:15) Jesus made it clear that as we love Him and do His will we will experience the indwelling presence. "All those who love me will do what I say. My Father will love them, and we will come to them and live with them. (John 14:23) Because you have the Spirit of God living on the inside of you, Paul assures you that "God is working in you, giving you the desire to obey him and the power to do what pleases him." (Phil 2:13)

When you face trials and tests, know, as John wrote that "You belong to God, my dear children...the Spirit who lives in you is greater than the spirit who lives in the world." (1 John 4:4) Christ on the inside of you is greater than any force of the enemy or any spirit of disobedience. Jesus overcame the spirit of disobedience. You too can overcome by the Christ that indwells you. As Paul wrote, "If God is for us, who can ever be against us?" (Rom 8:31) When you miss it, all you have to do is to repent of your mistake and God is faithful to put you back on track. (1 John 1:9)

Faithfulness to do the will of God is hard to find these days. We must not let the laziness of other believers around us be the standard of our faithfulness to Christ. The ruler by which we measure faithfulness is found only by looking at the faithfulness of Christ.

Here are 12 promises for the Christian to claim:

- God's presence -- "I will never leave thee" (Heb. 13:5)
- God's protection -- "I am thy shield" (Gen. 15:1)
- God's power -- "I will strengthen thee" (Isa. 41:10)
- God's provision -- "I will help thee" (Isa. 41:10)
- God's leading -- "And when He putteth forth His own sheep, He goeth before them" (John 10:4)
- God's purposes -- "I know the thoughts that I think toward you, saith the Lord, thoughts of peace, and not of evil" (Jer. 20:11)
- God's rest -- "Come unto Me, all ye that labor and are heavy laden, and I will give you rest" (Matt. 11:28)
- God's cleansing -- "If we confess our sins, He is faithful and just to forgive us our sins, and to cleanse us from all unrighteousness" (1 John 1:9)
- God's goodness -- "No good thing will He withhold from them that work uprightly" (Psalm 84:11)
- God's faithfulness -- "The Lord will not forsake His people for His great name's sake" (1 Sam. 12:22)
- God's guidance -- "The meek will He guide" (Psalm 25:9)
- God's wise plan -- "All things work together for good to them that love God" (Rom. 8:28)

SOURCE: Our Daily Bread, January 1, 1985.

May you develop and cultivate the fruit of faithfulness in your life as you become more conscious of God's presence in you.

Prayer Points:

- Father, thank You that You are a faithful God.
- That in You there is no shadow of turning.
- Thank You for reminding me that the heaven and earth will pass away but Your Word will never pass away.
- May I develop the fruit of faithfulness to You and to Your Word.

In Jesus' Name.
Amen

Verse for the Day:

"God is working in you, giving you the desire to obey him and the power to do what pleases him." (Phil 2:13)

Blessed Are The Meek!

- Meekness is not weakness.
- Blessed are the meek, for they shall inherit the earth.

"But the fruit of the Spirit is....meekness" Gal 5:22, 23

Many people know that Jesus was 'meek'. The Bible refers to Moses as 'the meekest man on the face of the earth'. (Num 12) Many think that 'meekness' means being a doormat, or being able to suffer abuse without resorting to any form of retaliation. Meekness has a three part definition:

A person who is meek is:
1. self-controlled or slow to give or take offence,
2. humble in spirit and lowly in mind, and
3. teachable.

Today we will look at the first function of the fruit of meekness in the life of a believer, being able to exercise self control or being slow to take offence. Many believers consider themselves meek if they do not take offence when they are reprimanded for their wrong actions. It is not an opportunity for exhibiting meekness, when a person who is at fault suffers the consequences of his own mistakes or misdeeds. "For it is commendable if a man bears up under the pain of unjust suffering because he is conscious of God. But how is it to your credit if you receive a beating for doing wrong and endure it? But if you suffer for doing good and you endure it, this is commendable before God. To this you were called, because Christ suffered for you, leaving you an example that you should follow in his steps." (1 Peter 2:19,20)

Smooth words create an atmosphere of gentleness that heals roughness and bitterness.

Meekness is displayed when a person does not take offence when he or she suffers for being in the right. They do not react negatively even when they are being falsely accused, slandered, afflicted or persecuted. The strength to exercise self control while suffering injustice comes from cultivating the fruit of meekness. Moses was a good example when he was spoken against by Aaron and Miriam who questioned his fitness to fulfil the role of spiritual authority God had placed him in. Moses did not defend himself, but God came to his defence, rebuked his persecutors and vindicated him before their very eyes. Moses exercised self control and did not retaliate. God's desire is that we do not repay evil for evil, but turn occasions for offence into opportunities for intercession.

When Moses came down the mountain from receiving the tablets of the Ten Commandments, he found the children of Israel worshipping a golden calf. He dropped the tablets in anger, but composed himself and fell back on his face before the Lord and fasted for forty more days and nights on behalf of the people. The Bible tells us, "The Lord's servant must not quarrel; instead, he/she must be kind to everyone, able to teach, not resentful. Those who oppose him/her, he/her must gently instruct, in the hope that God will grant them repentance leading them to a knowledge of the truth, and that they will come to their senses and escape from the trap of the devil, who has taken them captive to do his will." (2 Tim 2:24-26)

Meekness is an essential quality that God requires of those who serve Him as He knows you will always encounter opposition and persecution. "Yea, and all that will live godly in Christ Jesus shall suffer persecution." (2 Tim 3:13)

You are the light and the salt of the earth. Your testimony or witness is vital to the lost and dying world. May you develop the fruit of meekness in your life to help you overcome being offended at persecution and opposition to the Word that you face.

Prayer Points:

- Father, thank You for showing me through Your Word that the fruit of meekness is important to my life.
- Help me to understand why I need to cultivate and develop it within my life.
- Help me to exhibit the fruit of meekness today.

In Jesus' Name.

Amen

<u>Verse for the Day</u>:

"Therefore, as the elect of God, holy and beloved, put on tender mercies, kindness, humility, meekness, longsuffering." (Col 3:12)

Meekness: What About Others! (2)

* Meekness is defined as not occupied with self.
* Blessed are the meek, for they shall inherit the earth.

"But the fruit of the Spirit is….meekness" Gal 5:22, 23

The second function of meekness enables believers to be humble in spirit and lowly in mind. Bible scholar W. E. Vine defines meekness as "the opposite to self-assertiveness and self-interest; it is not occupied with self at all. Meekness = Humility.

"Do nothing out of selfish ambition or vain conceit, but in humility consider others better than yourselves. Each of you should look not only to your own interests, but also to the interests of others." (Phil 2:3-4) Is the welfare of others more important than your own? Moses esteemed others so much more highly than himself that he was willing to offer his own salvation on their behalf.

"The next day Moses said to the people, "You have committed a terrible sin, but I will return to the LORD on the mountain. Perhaps I will be able to obtain forgiveness for you." So Moses returned to the LORD and said, "Alas, these people have committed a terrible sin. They have made gods of gold for themselves. But now, please forgive their sin--and if not, then blot me out of the record you are keeping." (Ex 32:30-32)

Jesus was our perfect example of humility. Graham Kendrick wrote in his song:
"Meekness and majesty, human and deity,
in perfect harmony the one who is God.
Lord of eternity dwells in humanity,
kneels in humility and washes our feet.
Wisdom unsearchable, God the invisible,
love indestructible in frailty appears,
Lord of infinity, stooping so tenderly
lifts our humanity to the heights of his throne.
O what a mystery. Meekness and majesty.
Bow down and worship, for this is your God."

Dr. Samuel Brengle of the Salvation Army said "The axe cannot boast of the trees it has cut down. It could do nothing but for the woodsman. He made it, he sharpened it, and he used it. The moment he throws it aside, it becomes only old iron. O that I may never lose sight of this."

The first barrier to meekness arises whenever we claim as our own what is really a gift of God. To live in meekness, we must try to remember that all we are, have, and can do is a gift. It is an act of arrogance to place ourselves at the centre of being and doing. Only God belongs there. Arrogance is the opposite of humility. It compels us to treat our limits not as unique openings through which God can reveal his goodness but as diseases to be cured.

"Brethren, if a man be overtaken in a fault, ye which are spiritual, restore such an one in the spirit of meekness; considering thyself, lest thou also be tempted." (Gal 6:1) Paul specifies the attitude and conduct God expects His children to display toward those who have been 'overtaken in a fault'. Vine tells us that the Greek word translated 'restore' in this verse, means 'to mend, to furnish completely'. It is only with the fruit of meekness that believers will be prepared to lay down their lives and allow the spirit of meekness to manifest itself in them so they may keep going and keep restoring one another. True meekness requires effort continuously.

Prayer Points:

- Father, may I cultivate the fruit of meekness in my life.
- May I think of the welfare of others and not just of myself.
- Help me to exhibit the fruit of meekness today.

In Jesus' Name.
Amen

Verse for the Day:

"Therefore, as the elect of God, holy and beloved, put on tender mercies, kindness, humility, meekness, longsuffering." (Col 3:12)

Day 32

Meekness: How Teachable Are You? (3)

- Meekness is not some special anointing. It must be cultivated and developed.
- Blessed are the meek, for they shall inherit the earth.

"But the fruit of the Spirit is….meekness" Gal 5:22, 23

Having the fruit of meekness in your life enables you to be teachable.

"So get rid of all the filth and evil in your lives, and humbly accept the message God has planted in your hearts, for it is strong enough to save your souls." (James 1:21) The only way that you will endure to the end, overcome and not be overtaken is through having a teachable spirit.

One of the greatest obstacles to you developing a teachable spirit is the 'traditions of men'. Jesus said to the Pharisees and scribes concerning this problem, "You break the law of God in order to protect your own tradition. And this is only one example. There are many, many others." (Mark 7:9) The dictionary defines *tradition* as 'the handing down of statements, beliefs, legends, customs, behavioural patterns etc. from generation to generation, especially by word of mouth or example. To me, 'traditions of men' is simply 'anything that is not in line with the Word and Spirit of God.' Even in the Pentecostal, charismatic and full gospel churches, there are traditions that become obstacles to saints developing a teachable spirit.

Jesus is coming back for people who are holy, without blemish, without spot, and without any such thing. How are these people going to get this way? Ephesians 5:25, 26 reveals how spotlessness is achieved in our lives: Jesus "gave up his life for her to make her holy and clean, washed by baptism and God's word." (Eph 5:26) The teaching, preaching, admonishing and exhorting of the word of God is what will bring the Church of Jesus Christ into proper doctrine, thereby washing us, cleansing us, and renewing our minds. "All Scripture is inspired by God and is useful to teach us what is true and to make us realize what is wrong in our lives. It straightens us out and teaches us to do what is right. It is God's way of preparing us in every way, fully equipped for every good thing God wants us to do." (2 Tim 3:16-17)

A believer who is not meek is in danger of becoming 'traditional', meaning that the Word of God will be of no effect in their lives. They will resist or refuse to accept instruction, doctrine, correction and rebuke when it is not what they want to hear.

May you develop the fruit of meekness s in your life so that we will be teachable and capable of receiving the glorious truth of the Word of God. May you be prepared to change your 'pet doctrines' if the Lord tries to give you His full counsel. The Spirit of truth will guide believers into all truth if they are teachable enough for Him to do so. A glorious church without spot must be a church that is obedient to the full counsel of God.

The Lord wants to work meekness within you so He can one day hand over to you the sceptre of righteousness and make you ruler over many things. (Matt 25: 21,23)

Prayer Points:

- Father, may I cultivate the fruit of meekness in my life.
- May I remain teachable so I may receive all that You have for my life.
- Help me to exhibit the fruit of meekness today.

In Jesus' Name.
Amen

Verses for the Day:

"When the Spirit of truth comes, he will guide you into all truth. He will not be presenting his own ideas; he will be telling you what he has heard. He will tell you about the future. He will bring me glory by revealing to you whatever he receives from me. All that the Father has is mine; this is what I mean when I say that the Spirit will reveal to you whatever he receives from me." (John 16:13-15)

Day *33*

Help! I Want To Be Meek! (4)

- Meekness is not a gift, but a fruit to be cultivated.
- Are you prepared to pay the cost required?
- How can I develop the fruit of meekness in my life?

A person who is meek is self-controlled or slow to give or take offence, humble in spirit and lowly in mind, and teachable.

How am I going to develop this fruit of meekness in my life? Here are three ways to do just that.

Fasting is one way to cultivate this fruit. David said, "I humbled my soul with fasting". (Ps 35:13) Fasting means 'abstinence from food'. Food is one of the enemy's most effective tools in causing people to stumble and miss out on God's perfect plan. A few examples are Adam and Eve (Gen 3:6), the children of Israel (Ex 16:3), Esau (Heb 12:16) and even Jesus was tempted with food by the devil. (Matt 4:3) It is said that 'the way to a man's heart is through his stomach.' Fasting produces sensitivity to the leading and things of the Spirit of God and displays a heart of compassion when used on behalf of others. (Is 58:6, 12) Isaiah says, 'a believer who fasts will be called 'the repairer of the breach' and 'the restorer of paths to dwell in'. These kind of people make a real difference to the world.

Another way is by benefiting from the wilderness experiences of life. Even though Moses was knowledgeable in the language and culture of Egypt, a type or symbolic representation of the world, after forty years in the wilderness, he was no longer self sufficient even with all his knowledge. Wilderness experiences have a way of humbling people. Paul wrote of Jesus, "Though he were a Son, yet learned he obedience by the things which he suffered." (Heb 5:8) Obedience can be defined as 'having a disposition to yield to others.' Coming to a place of yielding oneself to other people is the very basis of meekness. God allowed the children of Israel to go through the wilderness to learn humility. "Remember how the LORD your God led you through the wilderness for forty years, humbling you and testing you to prove your character, and to find out whether or not you would really obey his commands. Yes, he humbled you by letting you go hungry and then feeding you with manna, a food previously unknown to you and your ancestors. He did it to teach you that people need more than bread for their life; real life comes by feeding on every word of the LORD." (Deut 8:2, 3) What wilderness are you walking through now? Use it as a stepping stone to developing the fruit of meekness.

The third way for you to develop the fruit of meekness is through denial of self. Meekness is the opposite of self interest. Moses denied himself when he refused to be identified as a member of the ruling house of Egypt. (Heb 11:24). This was also true of Jesus. "Your attitude should be the same that Christ Jesus had. Though he was God, he did not demand and cling to his rights as God. He made himself nothing; he took the humble position of a slave and appeared in human form. And in human form he obediently humbled himself even further by dying a criminal's death on a cross." (Phil 2:5-8) Like Moses and Jesus, you must decide between living for self or living to do the will of God. Jesus submitted unconditionally to the Spirit of His Father within and the result of this was that the Spirit of God was given to Him without measure. (John 8:28-29; 3:34) Yielding is not something one does, it is an attitude of the heart. Yielding is the absence of resistance. It is the absence of an expression of self-will and it is an affection of the heart. In Christ, you are dead to the things of the earth and must quickly yield to the things of the Spirit and set your affections on things above. Then you will be made fit vessels for the Master's use. (2 Tim 2:20,21)

"Blessed are the meek: for they shall inherit the earth. (Matt 5:5) Our Lord is in the process of preparing the hearts of believers to whom He will hand over the rulership and the dominion of this earth, but He can only give that power and authority to the meek. Those who refuse to cultivate and develop the fruit of meekness will never experience the full benefits of the overcoming life.

Prayer Points:

- Father, help me to do the things that help me develop the fruit of meekness.

- May I yield to the experiences that you allow me to go through to draw me closer into the image of Jesus.
- May I have the attitude that Christ had and live to do Your will.
- Help me to exhibit the fruit of meekness today.

In Jesus' Name.
Amen

Verses for the Day:

"Since you have been raised to new life with Christ, set your sights on the realities of heaven, where Christ sits at God's right hand in the place of honour and power. Let heaven fill your thoughts. Do not think only about things down here on earth. For you died when Christ died, and your real life is hidden with Christ in God." Col 3:1-3

Self Control: His Power Within! (1)

- The fruit of self-control will enable us to crucify the flesh.
- This power will surpass all previous, unsuccessful attempts at self improvement.
- It is foolish to replace self-control with abstinence: the latter is good; the former is best.

"But the fruit of the Spirit is temperance: against such there is no law." (Gal 5:23) Temperance is translated 'self control' or 'continence' derived from strength, also translated power in the second half of Ephesians 1:19-20: "I pray that you will begin to understand the incredible greatness of his power for us who believe him. This is the same mighty power that raised Christ from the dead and seated him in the place of honour at God's right hand in the heavenly realms." The same strength and power that raised Jesus from the dead and exalted Him in heaven is available to us as Christians today as a fruit of the Spirit which we may cultivate and develop in our lives.

The fruit of self-control will enable us to crucify the flesh and fulfil Galatians 5:24: "Those who belong to Christ Jesus have nailed the passions and desires of their sinful nature to his cross and crucified them there." Michael G. Moriarty in his book, 'The Perfect 10: The Blessings of Following God's Commandments in a Post Modern World' wrote, "The application of misplaced desires eventually becomes a cycle of addiction where stimulating encounters, relief, and the mad search for new experiences become ingrained in the recesses of the mind. The insatiable appetite to acquire, to own, to indulge, to take pleasure, to consume, is relentless. Rationality and moral self-control are dominated by the rising lust for power, an insidious power that becomes a sacred goal, a wholly consuming interest."

God, by His great love for us, has, through the fruit of the Spirit provided us with a supernatural seed of strength and self control. This seed requires cultivation to produce overcoming power by the Spirit. This power will surpass all previous, unsuccessful attempts at self improvement and will overcome any area of lust in the lives of those who possess and apply it. Paul wrote, "Remember that in a race everyone runs, but only one person gets the prize. You also must run in such a way that you will win. All athletes practice strict self-control. They do it to win a prize that will fade away, but we do it for an eternal prize. So I run straight to the goal with purpose in every step. I am not like a boxer who misses his punches. I discipline my body like an athlete, training it to do what it should. Otherwise, I fear that after preaching to others I myself might be disqualified." (1 Cor 9:24-27)

In order to live up to the expectations of God, a believer must have so much control over their body as to make it their slave. A body brought into subjection must be obedient to its owner. When the Spirit of God dominates a person, He demands of that person self control. As a result of this you will crucify the affections and lust of your flesh that wars against the Spirit.

Paul made an example of the children of Israel who lacked self-control although they experience mighty manifestations from God such as the parting of the red sea, eating of the spiritual meat and drinking of the spiritual rock, the cloud by day and the pillar of fire by night. They displeased God because they allowed themselves to be overcome of their own lusts during their trials in the wilderness. (1 Cor 10:1-13)

Paul writes from verse 6, "These events happened as a warning to us, so that we would not crave evil things as they did or worship idols as some of them did. For the Scriptures say, "The people celebrated with feasting and drinking, and they indulged themselves in pagan revelry." And we must not engage in sexual immorality as some of them did, causing 23,000 of them to die in one day. Nor should we put Christ to the test, as some of them did and then died from snakebites. And don't grumble as some of them did, for that is why God sent his angel of death to destroy them. All these events happened to them as examples for us. They were written down to warn us, who live at the time when this age is drawing to a close. If you think you are standing strong, be careful, for you, too, may fall into the same sin. But remember that the temptations that come into your life are no different from what others experience. And God is faithful. He will keep the temptation from becoming so strong that you can't stand up against it. When you are tempted, he will show you a way out so that you will not give in to it."

May you stand strong by the power of the Holy Spirit that dwells within you today.

Prayer Points:

- Father, thank You for revelation knowledge.
- Thank You for showing me that the same mighty power that raised Christ and exalted Him dwells within me.
- Help me to understand the power of the Holy Spirit at work within me today.
- May I walk in the fruit of self control today.

In Jesus' Name.
Amen

Verses for the Day:

"If you think you are standing strong, be careful, for you, too, may fall into the same sin. But remember that the temptations that come into your life are no different from what others experience. And God is faithful. He will keep the temptation from becoming so strong that you can't stand up against it. When you are tempted, he will show you a way out so that you will not give in to it." (1 Cor 10:12-13)

Self Control vs. Covetousness! (2)

- What has covetousness got to do with self-control?
- Me? Covetous? What are you talking about?

In the Old Testament God commanded His people not to bow down and serve idols. "You shall not make for yourself a carved image-- any likeness of anything that is in heaven above, or that is in the earth beneath, or that is in the water under the earth; 5you shall not bow down to them nor serve them. For I, the LORD your God, am a jealous God, visiting the iniquity of the fathers upon the children to the third and fourth generations of those who hate Me," (Ex 20:4-50

The Hebrew word translated 'serve' means 'to work' (in any sense); enslave; keep in bondage. It is true that not too many believers today are tempted with idolatry in the sense of bowing their knee before an idol. However, Paul wrote, "Therefore put to death your members which are on the earth: fornication, uncleanness, passion, evil desire, and covetousness, which is idolatry." (Col 3:5) Covetousness is the same as idolatry. Many of us are tempted with idolatry in the sense of serving whatever one has come to 'idolise in their lives. Whatever you 'work' for; whatever 'enslaves' you; whatever keeps you 'in bondage', that is an 'idol'.

Paul writing to Christians said, "You can be sure that no immoral, impure, or covetous person will inherit the Kingdom of Christ and of God. For a greedy person is really an idolater who worships the things of this world." (Eph 5:5)

The most common ways in which we are tempted to serve 'idols' in our lives are through our actions, thoughts and feelings. The degree of idolatry' in a Christian's life may be measured by the amount of time you devote to the coveting and pursuit of other things other than the things of God. How much time do I spend working and worrying about achieving some goal to attain some position or to obtain some desired object? How much time do we spend indulging ourselves in the blessings God has already provided in our lives? Jesus said, "You must worship the Lord your

God; serve only him." (Matt 4:10) Worship and service can be measured as much by time as by effort and service. If you are not careful to be self controlled in all things, you may end up serving the provision rather than the Provider. (1 Cor 9:25)

What are some of God's provisions that people end up serving instead of serving God?

- Food – Give us this day our daily bread, not our daily bakery. (Matt 6:11)
- Sleep – God gives His beloved sleep although to the self indulgent beloved one is asked, "How long wilt thou sleep, O sluggard? When wilt thou arise out of they sleep?" (Prov 6:9)
- Prosperity – God takes pleasure in the prosperity of His servant. (Ps 35:27) However Jesus warns us in Matt 6:24, "No one can serve two masters. For you will hate one and love the other, or be devoted to one and despise the other. You cannot serve both God and money."

The fruit of self control helps us moderate our actions, thoughts and feelings, even in regard to God's provision. This is so important because Jesus warned, "Watch out! Don't let me find you living in careless ease and drunkenness, and filled with the worries of this life. Don't let that day catch you unaware, as in a trap. For that day will come upon everyone living on the earth." (Luke 21:34-35)

Today, may you cultivate the fruit of self control so you life will not be over indulgent and you will be soberly aware of the coming of 'that day'.

Prayer Points:

- Father, may I exercise the fruit of self control in my life today.
- May my response to the people and environment around be seasoned with salt and the light of the Gospel of Christ?
- May I seek to influence others and not to be influenced by the world's norms and standards.

In Jesus' Name.
Amen

Verse for the Day:

"But you are not like that, for you are a chosen people. You are a kingdom of priests, God's holy nation, his very own possession. This is so you can show others the goodness of God, for he called you out of the darkness into his wonderful light." (1 Peter 2:9)

Day 36

Self Control – Love Not The World! (3)

- You are in the world but are not of this world.
- Don't you realize that friendship with this world makes you an enemy of God?
- Overcoming spiritual adultery.

Another function of the fruit of self control is to aid believers overcome fornication or overcome what the Bible refers to as 'spiritual adultery'.

Paul reminds us of the fate of the children of Israel, warning: "And we must not engage in sexual immorality as some of them did, causing 23,000 of them to die in one day." (1 Cor 10:8) The children of Israel were overcome in the wilderness by the lust of the flesh with its affections and desires. In spite of the mighty manifestations of God they had experienced, they displeased God because they allowed themselves to be overcome of their own lusts and fleshly desires during their trials in the wilderness.

In the eyes of God, friendship with the world is spiritual fornication: "You adulterers! Don't you realize that friendship with this world makes you an enemy of God? I say it again, that if your aim is to enjoy this world, you can't be a friend of God. Apostle John wrote, "Stop loving this evil world and all that it offers you, for when you love the world, you show that you do not have the love of the Father in you. For the world offers only the lust for physical pleasure, the lust for everything we see, and pride in our possessions. These are not from the Father. They are from this evil world. And this world is fading away, along with everything it craves. But if you do the will of God, you will live forever." (James 4:4)

Believers who love the world and find themselves engaging in her lust of the flesh, lust of the eyes and her pride of life, are committing spiritual adultery against the Father. Paul reminds us that the liberty we have been called to is not to be used as an occasion to the flesh, but by love we must use this liberty to serve one another. (Gal

113

5:13) Every believer has been set free, but not so you may do whatever you want to do, but so you, by the Spirit, can do what God desires for you to do. (2 Cor 6:14-17)

God wants His children to be a holy people. "But you are a chosen race, a royal priesthood, a dedicated nation, [God's] own purchased, special people, that you may set forth the wonderful deeds and display the virtues and perfections of Him Who called you out of darkness into His marvellous light. Once you were not a people [at all], but now you are God's people; once you were unpitied, but now you are pitied and have received mercy." (1 Peter 2:9-10) According to Titus, "For the grace of God has been revealed, bringing salvation to all people. And we are instructed to turn from godless living and sinful pleasures. We should live in this evil world with self-control, right conduct, and devotion to God"

You are in the world but are not of this world. The fruit of self control enables us to develop the necessary self control to live in this world and yet not be conformed to it.

Prayer Points:

- Father, may I exercise the fruit of self control in my life today.
- May my response to the people and environment around be seasoned with salt and the light of the Gospel of Christ.
- May I seek to influence others and not to be influenced by the world's norms and standards.

In Jesus' Name.
Amen

Verse for the Day:

"Do not be conformed to this world (this age), [fashioned after and adapted to its external, superficial customs], but be transformed (changed) by the [entire] renewal of your mind [by its new ideals and its new attitude], so that you may prove [for yourselves] what is the good and acceptable and perfect will of God, even the thing which is good and acceptable and perfect [in His sight for you].." (Rom 12:2 AMP)

Self Control – Don't Tempt Christ! (4)

- The fruit of self control enables believers to submit to the God ordained authorities in their lives.
- Self control helps to mortify the deeds of the flesh and live in harmony with God's plan and purpose for your life

How is it possible for New Testament believers to tempt Christ? Why would Paul write in the New Testament, "We should not tempt the Lord [try His patience, become a trial to Him, critically appraise Him, and exploit His goodness] as some of them did--and were killed by poisonous serpents." (1 Cor 10:9) They tempted Christ by speaking against rightful authority. "They began to murmur against God and Moses." Why have you brought us out of Egypt to die here in the wilderness?" they complained. "There is nothing to eat here and nothing to drink. And we hate this wretched manna!" So the LORD sent poisonous snakes among them, and many of them were bitten and died." (Numb 21)

Paul explained, "When you follow the desires of your sinful nature, your lives will produce these evil results: sexual immorality, impure thoughts, eagerness for lustful pleasure, idolatry, participation in demonic activities, hostility, quarrelling, jealousy, outbursts of anger, selfish ambition, divisions, the feeling that everyone is wrong except those in your own little group, envy, drunkenness, wild parties, and other kinds of sin. Let me tell you again, as I have before, that anyone living that sort of life will not inherit the Kingdom of God." One of the works of the flesh is divisions or 'sedition', defined as 'incitement of resistance to or insurrection against lawful authority'. The fruit of self control enables believers to submit to the God ordained authorities in their lives. The flesh may resist submission to and rebel against rightful authority, but self control will cause believers to mortify the deeds of the flesh and live in harmony with God's plan and purpose for their lives.

There are different types of authorities in ones life: governmental authorities, church authorities, family authorities and work-related authorities. The fruit of self control will aid you conform to the scripturally prescribed order of authority. By so doing you will be pleasing God rather than tempting Christ. (See verses regarding submitting to authority: Rom 13:1,2; Eph 5:22-23; Eph 6:1; Heb 13:17)

What Does It Mean To Submit? The Bible uses different words like 'hupotasso' which is a military term to get in line, or 'hupeiko' which means to withdraw, yield, submit and 'hupakouo', which is to listen, attend and obey. A special word is 'peitho', which means to be persuaded, or won over, used in Hebrews 13.7 and James 3.3. When you submit, it doesn't mean you become a doormat. You are freely making your opinions, your talents, your time and your resources available to those in authority to achieve the plans God has for that group of people. You are willing to get in line with the vision that God has given to the leadership and be won over to a way of doing things that might not always be your way.

Why is it sometimes hard to submit to authority?
- A sinful desire to "go it alone" can be traced back to the fall of Adam and Eve.
- We all want to be in control, even though we might not admit it.
- Fear, resulting from abuse by fathers, husbands, teachers, pastors etc.
- The absence of a father figure through death or divorce, or multiple 'fathers' has eroded honour and respect.

Les Norman says "The answer to abuse is not a "I have no use for authority" kind of attitude. A better way is to seek a legitimate Godly man or woman with authority whom you can trust, honour and respect. One who will love you, rebuild the broken walls and gain your confidence and trust."

The Benefits of Submission are:

- Inner peace and personal release
- Spiritual covering
- You will see strongholds come down
- You will be fulfilled from serving others
- You will make more friends

- You will see the reality of the nation, country, church or family visions unfold before your eyes.

Prayer Points:

- Father, may I exercise the fruit of self control in my life today.
- Help me recognise as godly authority the authorities you have placed in my life.
- May I by the fruit of the Spirit submit to them as You require of me.
- May I not 'tempt Christ' by my behaviour.

In Jesus' Name.
Amen

Verses for the Day:

"Remember your leaders, who spoke the word of God to you. Consider the outcome of their way of life and imitate their faith. Obey your leaders and submit to their authority. They keep watch over you as men who must give an account. Obey them so that their work will be a joy, not a burden, for that would be of no advantage to you." (Heb 13:7, 17)

Day 38

Self Control – Master The Tongue! (5)

- Ever felt you had good reason to murmur, grumble and complain about your situation?
- Nowhere in the Bible is it stated that unpleasant circumstances are an excuse for murmuring.
- How to use such periods of adversity to hold your tongue as you hold your ground.

Paul reminds us not to "discontentedly complain as some of them did--and were put out of the way entirely by the destroyer (death)." The children of Israel were guilty of complaining about their lot and their leaders. Both types of negative speech are condemned as being detrimental to the individual believer as well as the whole church.

How many times have we felt like they did: that we are justified as we grumble and complain about our situation? Every local body of believers finds itself in circumstances offering a greater opportunity or temptation to murmur than those in which the children of Israel found themselves. However, nowhere in the Bible is it stated that unpleasant circumstances are an excuse for murmuring.

According to James, the tongue is the one member of the body that is capable of defiling the whole body: "And the tongue is a fire. [The tongue is a] world of wickedness set among our members, contaminating and depraving the whole body and setting on fire the wheel of birth (the cycle of man's nature), being itself ignited by hell." (James 3:6) This is referring to the negative effect of speech on the individual believer.

The tongue is capable of corrupting the whole Body of Christ. "But if you bite and devour one another [in partisan strife], be careful that you [and your whole fellowship] are not consumed by one another." (Gal 5:15) The tongue is the worst enemy of the Church. It destroys from within. When we grumble and complain about our leaders or about each other, regardless of how justifiable our complaint might be, we are actually consuming or destroying one another. As a result, the whole body suffers. According to James, the flesh of man is not strong enough to put a stop to this destructive work of the tongue within the Body of Christ. "But the human tongue can be tamed by no man. It is a restless (undisciplined, irreconcilable) evil, full of deadly poison." (James 3:8)

The power necessary to control this potential source of corruption among believers must come from the Spirit of God as we individually cultivate and develop the fruit of self control. How can we do this? According to James, "We all make many mistakes, but those who control their tongues can also control themselves in every other way. We can make a large horse turn around and go wherever we want by means of a small bit in its mouth. And a tiny rudder makes a huge ship turn wherever the pilot wants it to go, even though the winds are strong." (James 3:2-4) Whatever our individual strengths or weaknesses, we can bring about a change in any area of our personal lives simply by controlling out tongues. Here are a few verses to meditate on about the power of your mouth. God said to Joshua, "Study this Book of the Law continually. Meditate on it day and night so you may be sure to obey all that is written in it. Only then will you succeed."

1) "If you keep your mouth shut, you will stay out of trouble." (Prov 21:23)
2) "You have trapped yourself by your agreement and are caught by what you said." (Pro 6:2)
3) "For it is by believing in your heart that you are made right with God, and it is by confessing with your mouth that you are saved." (Rom 10:10)
4) Everyone enjoys a fitting reply; it is wonderful to say the right thing at the right time!" (Pro 15:23)
5) "You brood of snakes! How could evil men like you speak what is good and right? For whatever is in your heart determines what you say. (Matt 12:34)
6) "Above all else, guard your heart, for it affects everything you do." (Pro 4:23)

Prayer Points:

- Father, thank You for showing me the power that my tongue has over my life.

- May I take the time to bring it under the control of Your Spirit.
- May I develop and cultivate the fruit of self control in my life so that I speak only that which I am to speak and no more.
- May I keep my tongue by keeping my heart pure as this affects my entire life?

In Jesus' Name.
Amen

Verse for the Day:

"We all make many mistakes, but those who control their tongues can also control themselves in every other way." (James 3:2)

Day 39

I Choose Self Control! (6)

- Walk in the Spirit and you will not fulfil the lust of the flesh.
- The Holy Spirit is your helper.

Paul wrote to the Christians in Galatia, "So I advise you to live according to your new life in the Holy Spirit. Then you won't be doing what your sinful nature craves. The old sinful nature loves to do evil, which is just opposite from what the Holy Spirit wants. And the Spirit gives us desires that are opposite from what the sinful nature desires. These two forces are constantly fighting each other, and your choices are never free from this conflict." As we are comprised of flesh and spirit, whichever one of the two we feed will be the one that will dominate and eventually become manifest in our lives.

I remember reading about a guy who stopped in the grocery store on the way home from work to pick up a couple of items for his wife. He wandered around aimlessly for a while searching out the needed groceries. As is often the case in the grocery store, he kept passing this same shopper in almost every aisle. It was another father trying to shop with a totally uncooperative three year old boy in the cart.

The first time they passed, the three year old was asking over and over for a candy bar. Our observer couldn't hear the entire conversation. He just heard Dad say, "Now, Billy, this won't take long." As they passed in the next aisle, the three year old's pleas had increased several octaves. Now Dad was quietly saying, "Billy, just calm down. We will be done in a minute." When they passed near the dairy case, the kid was screaming uncontrollably. Dad was still keeping his cool. In a very low voice he was saying, "Billy, settle down. We are almost out of here." The Dad and his son reached the check out counter just ahead of our observer. He still gave no evidence of loosing control. The boy was screaming and kicking. Dad was very calming saying over and over, "Billy, we will be in the car in just a minute and then everything will be OK."

The bystander was impressed beyond words. After paying for his groceries, he hurried to catch up with this amazing example of patience and self-control just in time to hear him say again, "Billy, we're done. It's going to be OK." He tapped the patient father on the shoulder and said, "Sir, I couldn't help but watch how you handled little Billy. You were amazing." Dad replied, "You don't get it, do you?" I'm Billy!"

Paul described the battle between his flesh and his spirit that went on within him as his body and his regenerated spirit rages against each other. (Rom 7:14-25). He acknowledges that the only one who will deliver him from this battle is Jesus Christ our Lord.

As you yield to the Spirit of God within, you will develop the strength you need to exercise control over your flesh and to bring it into submission to your re-born spirit. As this strength and control increases, so will the fruit of self control.

How do we strengthen our inner man?

1. Though assimilation of the Word of God: "So make every effort to apply the benefits of these promises to your life. Then your faith will produce a life of moral excellence. A life of moral excellence leads to knowing God better. 6Knowing God leads to self-control. Self-control leads to patient endurance, and patient endurance leads to godliness."
2. By speaking in tongues: "A person who speaks in tongues is strengthened personally in the Lord, but one who speaks a word of prophecy strengthens the entire church."
3. Through praise: "You have taught children and nursing infants to give you praise. They silence your enemies who were seeking revenge."

Receive the grace of God that provides you with access to the Father so you can approach Him at any time – day or night. Grace is defined as 'God's ability to do His will. God is there to help you in your time of need of self control.

Prayer Points:

Dear Lord,
I choose to be self-controlled.
I am a spiritual being. After this body is dead, my spirit will soar. I refuse to let what will rot, rule the eternal. I choose self-control. I will be drunk only by joy. I will be impassioned only by my faith. I will be influenced only by God. I will be taught only by Christ. I choose self-control.

In Jesus' Name.
Amen

Verse for the Day:

"So let us come boldly to the throne of our gracious God. There we will receive his mercy, and we will find grace to help us when we need it." (Heb 4:16)

Suzanne Nti is pastor of On Eagles Wings Church in Milton Keynes, United Kingdom. She is a wife, mother of four, lawyer, administrator, speaker and author to the Glory of God Almighty who called and equipped her.

OTHER BOOKS BY SUZANNE NTI

- GOD'S CALL TO WOMEN

- GOD'S ROEPING VOOR VROUWEN

- HIGHER THOUGHTS & HIGHER WAYS –
  One Year Devotional

- WALKING AWAY FROM COMPROMISE

To order:

By email: orders@freshmanna.org.uk or snti@freshmanna.org.uk

By phone: +44 (0)1908 528441
By fax: +44 (0) 1908 394752

By post: Fresh Manna
                P O Box 5083
                Milton Keynes MK7 7YY
                United Kingdom

Website: www.freshmanna.org.uk

For prayer email: prayer@freshmanna.org.uk